Conteography | Child Care Policy and | **Practice**

Contemporary Child Care Policy and Practice

Barbara Fawcett, Brid Featherstone
and Jim Goddard

First published 2004 by
PALGRAVE MACMILLAN
Houndmills, Basingstoke, Hampshire RG21 6XS and
175 Fifth Avenue, New York, N.Y. 10010
Companies and representatives throughout the world

PALGRAVE MACMILLAN is the global academic imprint of the Palgrave Macmillan division of St. Martin's Press, LLC and of Palgrave Macmillan Ltd. Macmillan® is a registered trademark in the United States, United Kingdom and other countries. Palgrave is a registered trademark in the European Union and other countries.

ISBN-13: 978-0-333-97379-0 paperback
ISBN-10: 0-333-97379-8 paperback

This book is printed on paper suitable for recycling and made from fully managed and sustained forest sources.

A catalogue record for this book is available from the British Library.

A catalog record for this book is available from the Library of Congress.

10   9   8   7   6   5   4   3   2
13   12   11   10   09   08   07   06   05

Printed in China

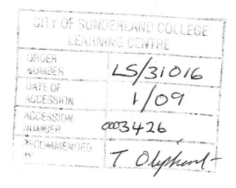

Dedicated to Kate and Sophie, Anthony and Áine

Contents

List of Tables, Figure and Box

Tables

Figure

Box

Acknowledgements

As always with a publication of this kind, the three authors have had help from a number of other people in the production of this book. Without their help, the book would have been a much harder task and a less complete work.

First, we would like to thank Sue Hanson at the University of Huddersfield for her sterling work in getting the manuscript into a finished state against fairly tight deadlines. We would also like to thank Professor Ruth Lister at the University of Loughborough, who provided helpful comments on an early version of the book. We have also benefitted from the feedback of academic colleagues at a seminar at the University of Huddersfield in February 2003 and at the Social Policy Association Annual Conference in Middlesbrough in July 2003.

Finally, we would like to thank Catherine Gray and Kate Wallis at Palgrave Macmillan, who have been unfailingly supportive as our work has proceeded.

List of Abbreviations

ACPC	Area Child Protection Committee
BV	Best Value
CAMHS	Children and Adolescent Mental Health Services
CPR	Child Protection Register
CSP	Children's Services Planning
DoH	Department of Health
LAC	Looked After Children
MAP	Management Action Plan
OFSTED	Office for Standards in Education
PSS	Personal Social Services
QP	Quality Protects
SSD	Social Services Department
SSI	Social Services Inspectorate
YOT	Youth Offending Team

CHAPTER 1

Introduction

> (A)ctivity in itself is not necessarily a good thing and it certainly does not always signify action of the kind desired by those in need of assistance, nor that advocated by reformers working on their behalf. (Hendrick, 2003, p. 252)

Recent years have seen increasingly high levels of government activity and intervention in the UK in the field of child welfare policy. As a result, it has been difficult for many policy activists and researchers to keep up with the pace of developments. It has also been difficult to discern common themes within the wide array of initiatives. In the early to mid-1990s, this was less of an issue. Although the Conservative governments had introduced a number of significant measures – such as the Children Act 1989, the Child Support Act 1991 and the Family Law Act 1996 – they were much less interventionist than their successors, the Labour governments elected in 1997 and 2001. This is evident from Table 1.1, which lists some of the key initiatives relating to children between 1998 and 2003.

Some of these measures apply to all children, some to specific groups. Also, many of these initiatives and others interact or overlap with each other. This can make for a confusing picture of a nevertheless fascinating period in child welfare policy. Our analysis seeks to reduce such confusion by focusing on common themes whilst also examining developments in specific areas. In what follows, we document *what* has been happening in recent years, and also *why*, in a range of child welfare policy areas: family policy, child protection, looked after children, youth justice, children with mental health difficulties, children with disabilities and children as carers.

Our focus on these areas is prompted by two considerations. First, they correspond with our areas of interest and expertise as

Table 1.1 Some significant policy initiatives with respect to children, 1998–2003

Year	Policy initiatives
1998	• National Childcare Strategy • Quality Protects (QP) initiative • Crime and Disorder Act (youth justice measures) • Guidance on the Education of Looked After Children • Supporting Families: A Consultation Document
1999	• Beveridge Lecture: pledge to abolish child poverty within 20 years, via National Minimum Wage, Working Families Tax Credit, Child Care Tax Credit, Tax Credit for Families with Children. • Protection of Children Act • Youth Justice and Criminal Evidence Act • Sure Start Programme
2000	• Cabinet Committee on Children and Young People's Services • Children (Leaving Care) Act • Care Standards Act • Carers and Disabled Children Act • Framework for the Assessment of Children in Need and Their Families
2001	• Special Educational Needs and Disability Act • Connexions Service
2002	• Adoption and Children Act
2003	• Minister for Children and Young People • Green Paper on Children at Risk • Children's Trusts • Child Trust Funds • Children's Bill • Children's Commissioner for England (from 2004)

authors. Secondly, explorations across such diverse policy and practice areas open up interesting and important possibilities for comparing and contrasting the constructions of children which motivate such developments. However, we also try to give due weight to the situation of children as a whole and their commonalities. Such considerations provide a context within which our more detailed discussions are conducted. For example, there have been extremely important developments in relation to tackling child poverty and the government has placed considerable emphasis on mainstream compulsory education. The first issue is explored from different angles both in this chapter and in some of the more detailed policy chapters. The second issue also receives some attention in this chapter and is explored in relation to developments around looked after children and children with disabilities.

In the light of the different policy fields discussed, the age range covered extends from pre-birth, the very early years of childhood in some cases (for example, Sure Start) up to 21 in others (for example, those who come under the new arrangements for leaving care). However, the vast majority of developments relate to children and young people under the age of 18. This raises an important issue in relation to the terminology used and, indeed, to the title of the book. The term 'child' is neither appropriate nor accurate in many instances. For example, in relation to youth justice we are concerned with the 10–17 age range. However, for the sake of brevity the term 'child' and 'children' are those most commonly used. The exceptions to this are generally those initiatives which exclusively relate to older children (such as Connexions and the Children (Leaving Care) Act).

The book is largely focused on developments in England, unless otherwise stated. Constitutional changes in the late 1990s have led to increasing policy diversity within the UK. Scotland, of course, has always had a separate legal system and a distinctively different approach to child welfare. Wales is now beginning to develop its own direction under the aegis of the Welsh Assembly. Northern Ireland also has different policy approaches to child welfare, as in many other areas, stemming from its particular (and still developing) constitutional arrangements. Developments in Scotland, Wales and Northern Ireland all merit their own, separate discussions in this area. However, including them in this book would unnecessarily complicate our wider analysis.

In this chapter, we locate New Labour's approach to children within its project to construct a 'social investment state'. This, we argue, helps to explain both *what* they have done and *why*. It helps to explain how recent policy both builds upon and extends a well-entrenched historical discourse about children as *investments* (Hendrick, 1994, 2003; Daniel and Ivatts, 1998). There are a range of analysts concerned to sketch out the contours of the 'social investment state' (Giddens, 1998; Jenson and Saint-Martin, 2001; Esping-Andersen, 2002; Lister, 2002). These differ in terms of their level of detailed exploration of the implications for children. Our concern is with the relevance of this trajectory for specific groups of children and also to children more generally. We argue that in this context:

- The social investment state supports strategies which invest in children as a whole.
- However, it lays particular emphasis upon particular stages of childhood (such as early years) and on particular groups of children. By default, therefore, some of the commonalities between children, particularly in relation to generational power relations, receive little attention.
- On the other hand, this approach does render certain groups of children and young people more visible, as recipients of both support and control strategies.
- The social investment state supports entrenched constructions of children which places particular emphasis upon them as 'investments' for the future rather than as subjects whose present well-being matters.
- Parents are constructed and appealed to as key allies in ensuring children's welfare (via a range of supportive and controlling strategies). The focus is on their responsibilities rather than their rights.
- There is a reluctance to locate, consider or appeal to children as subjects and, associated with this, a piecemeal approach to children's rights – particularly for those children cared for by their parents.

The social investment state

Tony Blair (1999), in his historic Beveridge lecture *signalling* a commitment to abolish child poverty within 20 years, argued that there needed to be a redrawing of the welfare contract around a focus on:

> work for those who can: security for those who can't. This means refocusing dramatically the objectives and operation of the welfare state. If the knowledge economy is an aim, then work, skill and above all investing in children become essential aims of welfare... a welfare state that is just about 'social security' is inadequate. It is passive where we now need it to be active. It encourages dependency where we need to encourage independence, initiative, enterprise for all.

A clear articulation of what this social investment strategy means has been provided by Giddens (1998), who argues that the key feature of such a state is 'investment in human capital wherever possible, rather than the direct provision of economic maintenance' (p. 117). Jenson and Saint Martin (2001), from Canada, have critically explored this approach in relation to developments in a range of Western countries. They argue that terms such as the social investment state have begun to circulate as a design for successfully linking concerns around economic and social cohesion and signal a paradigm shift away from the post-war welfare state. Whilst the old welfare state sought to protect people from the market, a social investment state seeks to facilitate the integration of people into the market. Taylor-Gooby uses different language but makes essentially the same point when he describes the modern UK liberal welfare state as 'designed both to support success in a flexible market system and to enhance citizen welfare, so that social policy buttresses rather than burdens the wealth-producing economy' (Taylor-Gooby, 2003, p. 1).

Individual security in such a context is viewed as resulting from a capacity to change. Thus there is an emphasis on investing in human capital and lifelong learning: 'The notion is that such investments will be more suited to the labour markets of global capitalism, in which job security is rare, and flexibility is highly valued. For its part, social policy should be "productivist" and investment oriented, rather than distributive and consumption oriented' (Jenson and Saint Martin, 2001, p. 5). For state spending to be effective and worthwhile it must not simply be consumed in the present but must reap rewards in the future. From this perspective, social welfare spending may legitimately be directed to objectives such as supporting and educating children (because they hold the promise of the future), promoting health and healthy populations (because they pay off in future lower healthcare costs), reducing the probability of future costs of school failure and crime by young people, and fostering employability. Spending for current needs, by contrast, needs to be cautious and targeted and is motivated not just by reasons of social justice but also by a wish to reduce the threat to social cohesion posed by those who are marginalised. Inclusion of the marginalised is a necessary area for current expenditure.

In one sense, there is nothing new about all of this. A 'social investment' rationale has often featured strongly in the development of child welfare interventions and has been central, for example, to the high priority that education has always had for the Labour Party. However, what is new is the degree of emphasis placed on this rationale and the number of initiatives that flow from this. Its centrality to New Labour's approach stems, in part, from it being, almost by definition, market-friendly. More general concepts of social justice, on the other hand, tend to be antagonistic or, at best, neutral towards markets. This does not mean that Labour is uninterested in social justice – actions such as the National Minimum Wage and improvements in provision for state pensioners indicate otherwise – but it does suggest that we need to focus more attention on the application of the social investment rationale if we are to adequately understand Labour's approach to child welfare reform. As Gordon Browne has put it, 'Children who grow up in poverty experience disadvantage that affects not only their childhood, but also their experience as adults and the life chances of their own children. Support for today's disadvantaged children will therefore help to ensure a more flexible economy tomorrow' (Budget Report, 2003, para. 5.4).

Lister (2003) argues that under New Labour there has been a genuine, unprecedented attempt to shift the social priorities of the state to investing in children. She notes, for example, that the real financial value of assistance for children under the age of 11 virtually doubled between 1997 and 2002. This has involved both a redistribution of resources and, more commonly, an emphasis on the redistribution of opportunities; such as those to enable parents, both men and women, to take up paid work. For example, Sure Start, which was introduced in 1998 for parents and children under four, is compatible with social investment approaches developed in other countries, such as Head Start in Canada (Jenson and Saint-Martin, 2001). It exemplifies many of the themes of such an approach, with its emphasis on early years learning and its fostering of employability. The financial commitment is considerable; according to the Government's own strategy document (Delivering for Children and Families, Strategy Unit, November 2002), there will be a combined budget for Sure Start, early years and child care that will rise to 1.5 billion by 2005/2006.

Broader action on child welfare: poverty and education

An analysis of the kind that we are pursuing demands exploration of wider developments in child welfare and cannot focus exclusively on developments in relation to specific groups of children. Accordingly, it is worth examining what has been happening in relation to the two main areas of universal child welfare policy, action on child poverty and approaches to mainstream education.

The widest application of Labour's social investment rationale can be found in its approach to child poverty. The pledge to abolish child poverty in 20 years (with poverty defined as household income below 60 per cent of the median) was followed by a Treasury commitment to halve poverty within 10 years and, in 2000, by a further commitment to reduce it by a quarter by 2004. The Government's fourth annual report on progress in its anti-poverty strategy (Department of Work and Pensions, 2002) showed a fall in relative, real terms and persistent poverty, including child poverty. Labour's policy is managing to significantly reverse what had been a substantial increase in child poverty in recent decades, perhaps the worst legacy of previous Conservative administrations. By 1996, there were 4 million children living in poverty in the UK, three times as many as 20 years previously (Gregg et al., 1999). From a baseline of 4.2 million children living in poverty in 1998/1999, the target for 2004/2005 was 3.1 million. By 2000/2001, the number of children living in poverty had reduced to 3.9 million (Barnes, 2003). Longer-term measures such as the Child Trust Funds of between £250 and £500 per child introduced in 2003, designed to pay for future education or training at 18, add to the more immediate impact of measures such as child tax credits.

Bradshaw's (2003) analysis shows that large national, regional and local variations in child poverty persist. Moreover, the risks of child poverty remain heavily concentrated in certain types of household; jobless households, those with lone parents, young mothers with four or more children in the household and the youngest child under 5, and those where either an adult or child in the household is disabled (Bradshaw, 2003, p. 170). Notwithstanding such qualifications, Labour's seriousness in tackling child poverty is the single most important background factor to all else that we discuss in this book.

Focusing on children as investments in this and other ways is, according to Esping-Andersen (2002), the only sustainable and socially desirable way forward for the enhancement of poor children's welfare and for fostering their future life chances. This is because the basic requisites for a good life increasingly depend upon strong cognitive abilities and professional qualifications which increase the likelihood of employment: 'Remedial policies for adults are a poor (and costly) substitute for interventions in childhood...since a person's job and career prospects depend increasingly on his or her cognitive abilities, this is where it all begins' (Esping-Andersen, 2002, p. 49). Moreover, Lister (2003) notes that Britain, in comparison with many other countries in Europe, has traditionally proved a very difficult place for children, and a discourse around investment in children offers fresh opportunities to mobilise for much needed state support and services.

It can be argued that such an approach runs the risk that children become a cipher for future economic prosperity, overshadowing the child as citizen and restricting discussion of their own voices and their present quality of life; constructing children as 'becomings' rather than 'beings' can obscure the importance of engaging with them as subjects in the here and now (Lee, 2001; Hendrick, 2003). However when children are asked about their experiences of poverty, their accounts reinforce the importance of eradicating such poverty (Ridge, 2002).

With respect to education, at the 1997 General Election Tony Blair identified 'Education, education, education' as the three top priorities for his government. It is curious, then, that so much of the Conservative legacy remains untouched by Labour. The biggest change came with early years education, with a focus on expanding nursery provision and reducing class sizes for 5-, 6- and 7-year-olds. There also been the introduction of literacy and numeracy hours. For older children, there was a focus on 'standards, not structures', so that there was very little attack on selection where it existed and an enhanced inspection regime through the Office for Standards in Education (OFSTED). Some Conservative initiatives were abolished, such as the nursery voucher scheme and the assisted places scheme (allowing some gifted children to be privately educated but paid for by the state), and there was a slimming-down of the National Curriculum. There were also new initiatives, such as Education Action Zones, Welfare Officers in schools to specifically tackle truancy and the 'Excellence in Cities' initiative.

Under Education Secretary David Blunkett, there was a considerable increase in spending on education and some successes. There was progress in reducing class sizes for the 5–7 age range, in expanding nursery education, in improved reading standards and in qualifications. However, there was a decline in pupil–teacher ratios at secondary level between 1997 and 2001 and debates continued about the negative impact of Standard Assessment Tests (SATs) on children in a more highly pressured compulsory education sector. New Labour has promoted a highly functional, future-oriented view of education (in further and higher education, as well as in the compulsory sector), so that:

> As with so much else in the relationship between New Labour and children, 'education' is not seen as a service for and on behalf of children, but as an arena in which children are to be trained for a variety of employments and status positions (Hendrick, 2003, p. 217).

As Hendrick also notes, what is new about the current focus of New Labour is the *centrality* that education attains in relation to its social and economic strategies. Both the changes it has made and its continuities with the Conservatives suggest that there has been a redefinition of the meaning and practice of education which has been considered and deliberate. This redefinition constructs education as being concerned with imparting predetermined sets of knowledge about obedience, skills and self-discipline to passive vessels. Despite the abolition of physical punishment in private schools in 1998 (largely a symbolic gesture, since it was little-used in the private sector by then), increasing central control has proved inimical to the development of children's rights to meaningful participation and involvement in mainstream education (Lansdown, 2001, p. 96; Jeffs, 2002, pp. 45–59; Tomlinson, 2003).

Parents, parental responsibilities and the rights of the child

Two features of policy under the Conservatives have been reinforced by New Labour. First, there is an emphasis on the responsibilities of parents to ensure their children's well-being, good behaviour and future outcomes. Secondly, there is a tendency to locate children solely within the confines of parent/child relationships. Research in the 1990s which indicated that 'poor parenting' (which could encompass a diverse range of issues) was a causal factor in children's criminality was highly influential with Jack Straw, Labour's future Home Secretary, and encouraged legislative developments such as Parenting Orders under the Crime and Disorder Act 1998 and a service infrastructure around parenting initiatives, financed partly through the Home Office. The key difference with the Conservatives, who also inscribed parental responsibilities within specific pieces of legislation (Fox Harding, 1997, 1999), was the periodic attempt by Labour to develop services for parents and children that reflect their rhetoric.

As a result, parents have been assigned a clear and expanding set of responsibilities alongside some supports.

Other continuities with the Conservatives are the continued uncoupling of parenthood and marriage and a pragmatic approach to the notion of family. This is illustrated by an emphasis on men retaining financial responsibility for children after marital breakdown and support for the view that co-parenting following divorce is the most desirable outcome for ensuring the welfare of children in such contexts. One of Labour's key objectives has been to support ways for parents to remain involved with, and responsible for, children regardless of whether they remain married to each other. This is evident from the broad policy approach of Labour's Ministerial Group on the Family (Adams, 2002, pp. 113–114). Whilst invariably posed in gender-neutral terms, this focus on parental responsibility can in practice have very different implications for men and women.

Alongside the focus on the responsibilities of parents, there is a marked reluctance to consider uncoupling children and parents in the sense of seeing children as actors in a variety of other settings and with a variety of influences. Moss *et al.* (2000) have argued that New Labour's approach overemphasises the role of parents in children's lives and actively militates against a policy climate which pays attention not only to children's own views, but also to the roles that children play in each others lives. For example, the welcome development of a National Childcare Strategy appears motivated largely by concerns to increase the ability of parents to enter the paid labour force rather than to improve the quality of life for children as a valuable activity in itself, or to recognise that children gain much from their engagement with other children and adults in a variety of settings beyond the home.

There is also a tendency to attach less importance to the development of consultation and advocacy processes for children living with parents. For example, a Children's Rights Director was appointed for looked after children under the Care Standards Act 2000. However, it was not until 2003 that plans were announced to appoint a Commissioner for all children. This was despite a previous policy commitment to do so under Blair's predecessor, John Smith, and considerable political pressure. Wales and Scotland had already appointed Children's Commissioners of their own (see Lansdown, 2001). Furthermore, there has been a reinforcement of the right of parents to smack their children, again despite considerable political pressure for change. This exemplifies a reluctance noted by some observers (for example, Lister, 2001), on the part of New Labour, to move away from a populist project which seeks to woo rather than lead. The failure to legislate against smacking indicates an unwillingness to challenge generational power imbalances and to signpost the need for more democratic practices between adults and children.

In general, the emphasis on parents and parental responsibilities does little to promote 'children's rights' as they are commonly perceived by activists in this area; as an approach which emphasises children as subjects, actors and citizens whose choices and autonomy should be respected (Harding, unpublished). Where government activism with respect to children's rights has increased, it has generally done so with respect to specific groups and categories of children – not towards children as a whole.

This caution is in spite of the fact that the last 30 years have witnessed an increasing interest not just in the rights and voice of children but also of other social groups. One illustration of this is that user-led political movements of welfare service recipients have emerged in fields such as physical disability, mental health and services for older people in recent decades and services have had to respond to these developments (Braye, 2000). Implicit in these developments is a greater concern with individual autonomy and choice.

The parallels between policy developments in relation to adults and those in relation to children are evident across a range of fronts. For example, the greater focus on the voice and involvement of children in the 1989 Children Act was paralleled by a greater focus on the involvement of other social services users through the 1990 NHS and Community Care Act. The development from that Act of client involvement in developing not only their own individual 'care plans' but also Annual Community Care Plans is now replicated, under Quality Protects (QP) and the Children (Leaving Care) Act 2000, with a stress on involving young people with respect to both individual decisions and also social services departmental-wide policy. However, it is apparent that there is much more willingness to offer such opportunities to children without, or living apart from, their parents. Where children are living with parents, there are considerable tensions between considering children as individuals in their own right, with their own voices, and engaging with children via their parents. Such tensions are sharply posed in relation to particular groups of children, such as those with disabilities. However, there are uneven and contradictory developments between differing government initiatives and departments. For example, Sure Start projects are obliged to involve and consult with parents but not children, whereas projects funded by the Children's Fund are expected to consult with children (see Jeffery, 2003).

Tackling social exclusion through targeting

How does discussion of 'social investment' relate to the more common and well-known rhetoric around 'social exclusion'? First, the latter represents a staging post away from social policy acting as a restraint on the market. Tackling social exclusion requires very different approaches to those adopted by past Labour governments seeking to achieve social justice. In some respects, it has a narrower focus. Labour has come to eschew large-scale attempts at social engineering in favour of a more targeted concern for the socially excluded, with marginalised groups in society, with the:

> significant minority of people cut off, set apart from the mainstream of society. Their lives are often characterised by long-term unemployment, poverty or lack of educational opportunity, and at times family instability, drug abuse and crime. (Blair, 1996, p. 141)

Whilst discussions of social exclusion have often focused on disabled people, low-paid workers, homelessness and the long-term unemployed, it is easy to see that significant groups of children and young people can be attached to these categories; either through their relationship to adults or in their own right. Concern over the welfare of children is a recurring theme in discussions of social exclusion, just as it is with the social investment thesis. It is therefore unsurprising that the first report of the post-1997 Labour government's 'Social Exclusion Unit' focused on truancy and school exclusion (Social Exclusion Unit, 1998a).

The importance of targeting is also a common feature of both the social investment and the social exclusion perspectives. The use of targeting is not only evident in relation to specific groups of children but is also often accompanied by the setting of specific targets within implementation strategies. This dual application of the concept of targeting is a constant feature of contemporary policy, as will become evident throughout the book. Some initiatives, such as QP, illustrate the tying-in of target-setting, funding and implementation (see Chapter 5). However, such target-setting can result in the achievement of targets in one area at the relative expense of other areas (Tunstill, 2000). Moreover most of the initiatives, such as QP and Sure Start, have short-term funding. This can result in the distortion of services to meet particular needs for specific periods of time. On the other hand, such target-setting offers positive possibilities for particular groups of vulnerable children. For example, looked after children and younger children are offered more opportunities to have their needs highlighted and addressed.

In summary, this overview has highlighted linked tendencies in contemporary policy on child welfare. Within a policy approach which has not only raised the profile of child welfare but also constructs children as investments, there is a considerable emphasis on recruiting parents as allies in ensuring children's welfare and a failure to consider children outside of the parent/child relationship. Furthermore, there is an emphasis on targeting and target-setting which can militate against a holistic approach to children and result in short-term approaches.

Structure of the book

The book sets out to explore particular policy areas in some depth and to consider the practice implications of developments in these areas. However, in line with our aim to locate policy developments within a wider context, Chapters 2 and 3 have a broader remit. In Chapter 2, we both consider important theoretical developments in the study of childhood and expand on some of the themes identified within this overview. First, we consider developments within the sociology of childhood which to date appear to have had a considerable impact upon the child welfare research agenda but much less impact upon policy developments. Secondly, recent theoretical constructions of the family – or, perhaps more accurately, deconstructions – are considered. Thirdly, these are reviewed alongside wider developments in relation to children's rights. The juxtaposition of these three discussions offers useful, if also problematic, insights into the contemporary constructions of children which underpin policy developments.

Chapter 3 considers the contested area of 'family policy'. As we have noted, this area has received considerable academic and political attention in recent years. The chapter provides an overview of 'family policy' under the Conservatives and New Labour and considers initiatives developed under New Labour in a range of arenas. It argues that to some extent a new era has emerged in that there is more of an emphasis on government support for families with children than there has been hitherto. However, it notes that universal approaches are largely bypassed in favour of targeted initiatives which are geared towards meeting the priorities of a social investment state, particularly in terms of reinforcing the responsibilities of parents to raise 'suitable' children.

The next set of chapters move us into specific policy arenas. They are designed to outline recent developments, explain how these developments can be understood and assess the implications they hold for child welfare practices.

Chapter 4, in examining the area of child abuse in the context of child welfare, considers an area of some relative legal continuity. Notwithstanding measures such as the Protection of Children Act 1999, the Youth Justice and Criminal Evidence Act 1999 and new guidance on assessment and working together, the Labour government has been largely content to rest on the legislative basis provided by the Children Act 1989. However, there has been a clear refocusing, in both welcome and unwelcome ways, of policy priorities. Exploring and tackling 'child abuse', as defined in the form of actions/inactions by adults including parents, appears to be less of a priority for government than tackling the risks posed to children's development by growing up in poverty or becoming involved in criminality. This is because it sits less centrally within a social investment approach. Indeed, 'risk' is increasingly defined in terms of the risk of social exclusion rather than, for example, of maltreatment by parents. This chapter explores the possibilities and constraints within the current policy landscape. It argues that an important casualty of the current climate is that there is little space for considering how child protection processes could be made more child-centred.

Chapter 5 is concerned with policy and practice developments with respect to looked after children. Such children were the subject of a number of significant initiatives by the 1997–2001 administration. In contrast to the invisibility of children who have been abused but remain under their parents' care, these children have been more highly visible. Whilst this activity was prompted by the emergence of evidence of failure with respect to both protection from abuse and in areas such as employment, education and housing, it is also the case that the problems experienced by such young people are relevant to wider issues of social cohesion. The chapter considers initiatives in areas such as educational support, quality of care and leaving care. Two key initiatives, QP and the Children (Leaving Care) Act 2000, are central to this discussion.

Chapter 6 considers youth justice policy. Youth justice as an issue came to occupy a central place in government policy in the late 1990s. The passage of the 1998 Crime and Disorder Act with a minimum of political controversy demonstrates the extent to which Labour had come to adopt the Conservative analysis and approaches. Much of the Act was concerned with youth justice issues and in this chapter we trace the origins of the Act and consider its implementation. We also consider other recent youth justice developments. Finally, we consider evidence on the effectiveness of recent approaches to youth justice and some of the problems associated with the underlying rationale that has guided these developments.

Chapter 7 examines the relationship of disabled children to three key areas. These are: social exclusion and citizenship, investing through parents, and investing in children. The chapter explores the opportunities, contradictions and constraints of the current policy context. In particular, it argues that disabled children have received much less attention than other groups of children considered in other chapters and that wider developments in relation to education may work against their welfare. We argue that whilst other initiatives in relation to poverty may offer much needed support, to be effective these need to be clearly linked to civil rights issues.

In Chapter 8, the position of children and young people with mental health problems is appraised. It is argued that both understandings of mental health and policy and practice directives relating to adults have a clear relevance for children and young people. The chapter explores the continued location of mental health provision within a predominantly medicalised framework, the implications for children and young people of a National Service Framework, and issues of rights and the potential for conflict between children, young people and their families. It is argued that current debates on mental health policy reform provide an opportunity to radically overhaul existing policies and practices and to develop initiatives that are responsive to the stated needs of children and young people with mental health problems.

Chapter 9 considers children and young people who operate as carers. As a group, such children have only relatively recently attracted attention from policy-makers. A range of perspectives operate in this area, with some viewing children and young people with caring responsibilities as being 'children in need' in relation to the Children Act (1989). Others have viewed such responsibilities as part of the give-and-take of family life and have emphasised heterogeneity rather than homogeneity with respect to family forms. Writers from within the disability movement, in particular, have taken exception to the implication that such caring relationships are straightforwardly onerous for the young person concerned and have emphasised reciprocity and different interpretations of 'caring'. Such perspectives, with their differing implications with respect to children's rights and the respective roles of the state and the family, are analysed in the context of the approaches taken by New Labour.

Finally, in Chapter 10, we consider the coherence, tensions and main features of contemporary approaches to child welfare. We return to the implications of the social investment approach and consider the broad features of current policy.

CHAPTER 2

Thinking About Children Today

Many features of the lives of children are shaped by social policy and their futures are central to its concerns. However, in much social policy and sociological literature they have remained relatively silent and invisible as subjects whilst also being the objects of considerable concern (for an overview, see Brannen, 1999). In recent years, this has begun to change. Researchers from a range of disciplines show an increased interest in rendering children visible and in exploring the contours of contemporary childhood(s). Developments in academic disciplines such as sociology and socio-legal studies, encompassed in the substantial ESRC Children 5–16 Programme, have opened up new fields of conceptual endeavour and applied inquiry in relation to childhood. These developments build upon and interlink with a decade of academic interest in – and pressure groups campaigning for – children's rights.

This chapter will outline the key themes which have emerged within these theoretical developments and which have led to what has been called a 'new paradigm' of childhood (Hill, 1997a). As well as highlighting the strengths and weaknesses of this new paradigm, it also relates the paradigm to attempts to 'deconstruct' the family. Finally, the most significant messages for policy-makers from this discussion are assessed. In particular, it considers Daniel and Ivatts' (1998) claim that the new paradigm poses a central challenge to social policies that are directed specifically at children – which are currently justified primarily in terms of their effect upon the future potential of the children concerned. Whilst a 'social investment state' is future-oriented, alternative approaches counsel the importance of seeing children as 'beings' rather than as 'becomings', and as people to be valued in their own right in the present rather than in terms of their potential as adults (Hutchinson and Charlesworth, 2000, pp. 576, 583–584).

This chapter differs from subsequent chapters in that the emphasis is largely on theoretical and conceptual debates. Whilst policy and practice implications are referred to where appropriate, these are developed more fully in relation to particular policy areas in the chapters which follow. Such theoretical concerns can be construed as somewhat superfluous in a book which focuses on policy and practice. However, it can be demonstrated that this is not the case. First, there is now a considerable literature on the role of ideas in the policy process (see John, 1998, pp. 144–166). Indeed, public policy can be primarily studied from just such a perspective (Heclo, 1974; Sabatier and Jenkins-Smith, 1993; Sabatier, 1999). In this context, one small example is offered to reinforce the point. The Department of Health's *Framework for the Assessment of Children in Need and their Families* (2000a) can be clearly seen – in the core document, the practice guidance (2000b) and the review of studies informing its development (2001) – to be significantly shaped by a range of psychological, sociological and social theories. The knowledge base used is eclectic, including psychodynamic, ecological and social learning theories (Department of Health, 2001a, pp. 17–29), but the links between theory and practice are open, acknowledged and encouraged. Secondly, our explanation of contemporary theoretical constructions of childhood will contribute to our overall analysis and explanation of contemporary policies in this area. If we are to detect any coherence or underlying themes in current policies towards children, we can do so only by engaging in theoretical debates about the nature of modern childhood.

'Discovering' children and childhood(s)

During the past two decades, sociologists have developed a significant interest in children (see, for example, Corsaro, 1997; James and Prout, 1997; Jenks, 1996; Smart *et al.*, 2001). In doing so, they have launched a considerable critique of their own discipline and have also singled out other disciplines (particularly developmental psychology) for criticism. The ESRC Children 5–16 Programme opens up questions about policies and practices in a variety of settings: in families of varying forms, in schools and public spaces, and in relation to topics as diverse as domestic violence, divorce, help-seeking, and computer use. Moreover, the programme also involved researchers from a range of disciplines beyond sociology (Children and Society, Special Issue, 2002).

Smart *et al.* (2001), who researched children's own accounts of family life after divorce as part of this programme, claim that the 'discovery of children' by sociology invites us to conceptualise children as creative and moral agents, with strengths and capabilities with which to shape their childhoods: 'Under this new paradigm children are transformed from unfinished projects under adult control to fully social *persons* with the capacity to act, to interact and to influence the social world' (Smart *et al.*, 2001, p. 2; italics in the original). This approach explicitly opposes approaches from within sociology and developmental psychology which construct children as projects and which are rooted in naturalistic models of childhood. In contrast to naturalistic models, the new 'sociology of childhood' argues that childhood is socially constructed and is not a natural or universal state arising from biology. Childhood appears here as a culturally variable concept (James and Prout, 1997). There is, therefore, not one childhood but many; whilst age may be relevant, particular differences in terms of gender, ethnicity, culture, socioeconomic status and familial contexts also become important areas of interrogation.

This argument opens up possibilities for exploring specific constructions of children in particular contexts and has consequently led to a plethora of such analyses (see, for example, Jenks, 1996; James *et al.*, 1998). Jenks notes that one powerful construction has been of children as little devils beset by original sin. Allied with this construction is the image of the savage or barbarian (see also Goldson, 2002). Such images are counterposed to that of the child as angel; naturally good and innocent. These notions of children as 'devils', 'savages' or 'angels' have, of course, a very long history (Cunningham, 1995). However, they also feature heavily in contemporary adult thinking and often operate as background noise when varying policy measures are being discussed. Throughout the 1990s, it was also apparent that there was an important gendered dimension to such discussions, with concerns about boys and young men very often lapsing into fears of innate barbarism or savagery (Coward, 1999).

A further influential model of childhood has been that of the embryonic child. This has also been the target of considerable criticism. It is argued that it is essentialist, assuming the child to have certain innate qualities. However, rather than being seen as inherently good or evil, children are presumed to be in an emergent state with pliable natures. If they have any social characteristics at all, they are said to be 'weak, fragile, unstable, irrational, deficient and capricious in both mind and body' (Smart *et al.*, 2001, p. 3). Moreover, this approach operates with a stages notion of children's development which emphasises their potential rather than their being and which clearly justifies both constraint and direction in the service of this potential. At its crudest, such a stages model can be characterised thus:

> Childhood is seen principally as a stage on the road to adulthood, which has a normative status. Childhood in relation to adulthood mirrors the primitive in relation to the civilised and the modern, the primate in relation to the properly human. This development is an inevitable and invariant process driven by a biologically rooted structure which the child inherits (Archard, 1993, p. 35).

Critics of this model are right to point out its power, but it may not be as essentialist as they portray it. Their view that developmental psychology ties the social nature of children to their biological growth and development fails to fully acknowledge the complexities of developmental psychology and the variety of theories within child psychology more generally. For example, an influential perspective within social work is attachment theory (Howe, 1995). Whilst it is complicated by the differential impact of attachment depending on age and it clearly ties later behaviour to early attachment experience, it also lays a central emphasis on exploring and facilitating *social* relationships for enhancing children's development. Also, within certain areas of developmental psychology the role of the child in interactions is recognised to be highly significant (Dunn and Deater-Deckard, 2001). As Corsaro (1997) notes, both Piaget and, in particular, Vygotsky placed great stress on the ways in which children construct their world in complex and, for the latter, highly active ways. Nor is it entirely accurate to characterise all of developmental psychology as operating with a 'stages' approach to children's development. Many contemporary developmental psychologists prefer to think in terms of sequences of development, thus capturing a sense of flexibility often missing in earlier notions of stages.

In our view, we should not be too quick to dismiss perspectives which take a developmental approach. Such perspectives may illuminate how children navigate their ways through childhood and manage crucial transitions as, indeed, some of their critics have acknowledged (Smart *et al.*, 2001). Whilst developmental perspectives which establish fixed notions of normality on children at particular stages are indeed problematic (and are recognised as such by many developmental theorists), it would be absurd not to recognise that competencies may differ with age. Some of the new thinking can lead to naivety about how competent specific children are, which can be irresponsible if we want to be alert to the ways in which children can be mistreated by adults. Thus the debate between such competing perspectives will have quite specific implications within the field of child protection. Emphasis on children as agents with capabilities can mask important differences between children. Growing awareness of the invisibility of abuse of children with disabilities, for example, alerts us to the importance of recognising that some children cannot make themselves heard for both physical and social reasons. Furthermore, there has been an unfortunate tendency within sociology to lump psychology and psychoanalysis together under the notion of the 'psy complex', with a consequent failure to interrogate key differences between and within these internally differentiated schools of thought and practice. Differing schools of psychoanalysis share very different views of children's 'nature' and of the importance of the 'social' in facilitating their development.

Nonetheless, psychological and psychoanalytic approaches can tend towards universal models of childhood and to perceiving children as 'potential' rather than as beings. Such embryonic models have particular implications for welfare practices and also inform common-sense understandings of children. Smart and Neale (1997) repeat a common criticism from within the new paradigm that this model, in seeing children as potential persons, locates them on the margins of social life (and, of course, citizenship), valued more for their future potential than their present existence. Corsaro (1997) makes essentially the same point in developing his own concept of 'interpretative reproduction'. By stressing the ways in which children creatively develop their own peer cultures in a social context and through appropriating material from the adult world, his critique is of the focus on children as future adults and of the individualist bias of much psychology. A view of children as potential persons can lead to presumptions that children are inferior to adults because they are not fully formed. As a consequence, adults may be presumed to be able to speak for children. In this way, children become invisible in academic and policy debates about their needs and interests. Sociology, for example, has traditionally tended to render children silent when studying families. Children have usually been viewed as acted upon rather than as actors. Historically, they have not been interrogated as research respondents in their own right in studies of how families operate. Within social policy, there has been a frequent failure to distinguish conceptually between children and families. Such approaches have been referred to as the 'familialisation of childhood' (Alanen, 1988).

In our view, fruitful research with children is best served by engaging with children's vulnerabilities as well as their capacities. Interestingly, in the research carried out under this new paradigm referred to earlier (ESRC Children 5–16 Programme), children themselves indicated that they did not wish to see themselves as unfettered free agents when they were asked about key developments in family life such as divorce. According to Prout (2001), in his overview of the messages emerging from the research programme, children emerged as reformists rather than revolutionaries when it came to having a say. For example, they wished to be involved in discussions in relation to post-separation living arrangements, but did not wish to be final decision-makers. An exclusive focus on children as free-floating actors runs the risk of burdening children and young people with responsibilities that they may feel unwilling and/or ill-equipped to shoulder. A concrete example concerns situations where children are experiencing maltreatment. Featherstone and Parton pose the question of how we devise systems and practices which are child-centred but which do not burden children with the responsibility of protecting themselves (Featherstone and Parton, 2001).

Children operate in specific and complex, often shifting, contexts and listening to what they say and think cannot be done in isolation from an exploration of the constraints and possibilities opened up by such contexts. The experience of ChildLine, a service run by adults but seemingly highly valued by children, cautions against assumptions that adult relationships with children are one-dimensional, defined by constraint and, moreover, that adult protection is not required by children (see MacLeod, 1999, for an outline of how ChildLine operates). These points will be returned to when discussing children's help-seeking behaviour in Chapter 4.

It is important to lay bare the social constructions of children which circulate in varying discourses and to open up spaces for children to be treated as valuable research respondents who can provide accounts of how they understand their social worlds. Furthermore, this can help to identify how such constructions of children illuminate the contemporary concerns of adults. For example, Jenks (1996) argues that, in a climate where adult partners come and go, in which class attachments have fragmented and there are fewer sources of belonging, adults can come to depend upon children as sources of stability. This, of course, is not merely a national phenomenon. Some have noted, with respect to the USA for example, that 'there has been a recent sharp rise in the sentimental and emotional value of children, as marital ties have weakened and become less significant in the lives of many adults' (Hutchinson and Charlesworth, 2000, p. 577). Moreover, there is tentative evidence that some fathers, in a world where traditional identities are destabilised, have come to invest in a more active fathering identity based upon developing strong relationships with their children (Featherstone, 2003).

Deconstructing 'the family'

Since the 1960s, there has been increasing criticism of analyses of family life which do not distinguish conceptually between the different members of families. Within sociology, there has been an almost complete abandonment of previously dominant functionalist analyses which treated the family as a unit and which assumed that the interests of individual members were complementary. From the 1960s onwards, women have been involved in naming the power relations which operate within particular family forms and which are premised upon male authority (often underpinned by the use of violence) and women's economic dependence. Putting it simply, they exploded the notion that all within the family were equal in terms of access to resources and speaking rights and opened the way for what has been called the 'democratisation of everyday life' (Giddens, 1992). This has involved a questioning of what was often taken for granted in terms of the division of labour within the private sphere and also a challenging of economic and emotional settlements which were premised on duty and self-sacrifice on the part of women. This challenging of domestic inequality has clearly had enormous implications for women, but it also opened up the possibility of children voicing their own concerns about their treatment within families.

Alongside feminist analyses of power within families, many of the developments from the 1960s onwards in relation to highlighting child maltreatment more specifically have been led by professionals.

Those within the medical profession initially focused on physical abuse (Parton, 1985). Furthermore, there have been important, if unevenly developed, spaces opened up – initially by adult survivors of child sexual abuse – for children to articulate their own concerns. However, whilst this is a process that is often led and supported by adult women, the interests of women and children cannot be presumed to coincide in this area. There has been an historical association, as Gordon (1989) documents, of women and children's attempts to challenge traditional patriarchal power relations, but there have also been important reminders that women also maltreat children and reproduce generational power imbalances (Featherstone, 1997). Moreover, it would be unwise to assume that there is or has been unanimity among women themselves and particularly among feminists about how they understand relationships within families and what they want to change. Black feminists have pointed out that state and societal racism have operated in ways which mean that 'family' has often been their refuge from a hostile world, and the recognition of violent and abusive behaviour by black men has often been tempered by understandings of how such black men are treated by the state (Mama, 1989).

The processes begun by adult women in relation to the democratisation of everyday life have led to calls for such processes to be extended to children (Beck and Beck-Gernsheim, 1995; Giddens, 1998). This democratisation is increasingly concerned not just with structural issues such as access to material resources, but also encompasses 'life politics' (Giddens, 1992; Ferguson, 2001). Life politics is concerned with questions such as 'how do I live?' and 'what do I want in terms of emotional connections with those around me?' It involves ongoing rethinking of identities and practices, especially emotional practices. The implications for relationships between men and women have been far-reaching. Women, it would appear, are increasingly unwilling to tolerate gendered emotional settlements which are not based upon discussion and give-and-take. Furthermore, the increasing diversity of family forms and the associated rethinking and negotiation which often accompanies changes in family forms mean that children need to acquire – and some are acquiring – new practical and emotional skills in order to navigate a new moral terrain encompassing fluid living arrangements and adult relationships (Smart et al., 2001).

The ties between children and parents have traditionally been regarded as exempt from the degree of voluntarism which characterises kin relationships generally. With respect to these wider kin relationships, Finch (1989) has argued that the degree of affection between kin rather than their positional relationships is central to determining what kinds of interactions occur between them. However, Smart *et al.* (2001) argue that this may now be becoming a feature of some parent/child relationships and have noted how often children in their research spoke of liking or not liking particular parents:

> They may have felt that their parents hold a unique position in their lives which could not be taken over in any absolute sense by other adults, but they no longer feel bound to them in the same way. We found that respect and liking significantly influenced the commitment as well as the closeness they felt towards them (p. 84).

Furthermore, an interesting study completed in the mid-1990s, which is unusual in that it asked children of varying ages what they needed from their fathers, found that older children held sophisticated views on the importance of respecting their fathers and they judged their fathers as worthy of respect or not according to their behaviour (Milligan and Dowie, 1998). This alerts us to the importance of recognising the pervasiveness of a culture of scrutiny in a post-traditional world. It is more and more difficult for individuals to justify behaviour on the basis of position or tradition and, with respect to the intimate and relational, the standards used to judge behaviour encompass emotional abilities as well as economic performance.

As indicated previously, a considerable degree of voluntarism has also crept into relationships between men and women, with women increasingly prepared to forego lives built upon notions of duty and tradition if they no longer feel that they are emotionally engaged with men (see Giddens, 1992). Whilst Smart and Neale (1997) have pointed out that this is not as straightforward as Giddens implies and that many women stay in unsatisfying relationships for the sake of children, Giddens is nonetheless highlighting an important tendency within modern relationships (Williams, 1999).

With regard to how adult women and men view relationships with children, the picture is very complex. It was not until the latter part of the twentieth century that any degree of space was offered to mothers to articulate ambivalence, either in relation to motherhood as an institution or in relation to actual children (Rich, 1976). According to Parker (1997), it has become harder for women to articulate ambivalent feelings in a climate where their lives have become more open-ended and less fixed. She argues that the more women's lives are changing, the more fixed become dominant definitions of femininity – of which being a loving mother is a central attribute. On the other hand, whilst ideals about being a good mother certainly remain very strong, they are clearly invested in by mothers rather than being merely imposed upon them. According to Coward (1993), the good mother today is not the stay-at-home mother but rather one who 'enjoys' mothering. As Kaplan (1992) notes, an historically unprecedented discourse on self-satisfaction and fulfilment has emerged in terrain which was dominated by concerns about self-sacrifice and duty. Mothers have access to a discourse on self-fulfilment even in this arena. This indicates a degree of voluntarism appearing even in the mother–child relationship. Whilst public articulation of ambivalence is rare, and furthermore there has been no big increase in mothers leaving children, there has been an increase in the numbers of women remaining childless (Bartlett, 1994). This is the other side of the same coin; women exercising choice about how best to live fulfilling lives.

What about men as fathers? Men have always had opportunities to opt out of the paternal role should they so wish. What is interesting in the contemporary UK is that many men appear to be refusing old models of fatherhood and embracing involved fatherhood models (see Henwood, 2002). The Child Support Act (1991) was a key step towards a policy approach which reinforces paternal responsibility and prevents men from opting out of financial responsibility. As we shall see in Chapter 3, considerable legislative and policy developments in the last decade have sought to enforce parental responsibility for both men and women as lifelong, binding and tied to biology. This constitutes an active repudiation of voluntarism in the parent–child relationship. However, if policy developments which seek to coerce families into supporting members who are old and incapacitated may be seriously out of line with what either party wishes, as Finch argues (1989), then policy developments which seek to enforce parental responsibilities in the absence of ascertaining the wishes of those involved, including children, may also be problematic in this respect.

In summary, theoretical, social and political developments have legitimised the deconstruction of the 'family' and continued a process of questioning paternal and adult power relations. They have also articulated the need for children to be consulted and listened to. Fox Harding's integrated discussion of the struggles within the construction of child welfare policy in the UK in recent decades (1997) illustrates this. However, as she reminds us, it is over-simplistic to see this in terms of a struggle between paternalism and objectification on the one hand and a rights perspective and the subjectivity of children on the other (her own approach acknowledges four different perspectives, of which these are only two). Nor is it easy to see anything linear in these struggles, even though the growth of interest in children's rights is a particularly prominent development and has shifted the debate about children in relation to both public policy and family (see Freeman, 1993, 1996; Hodgkin, 1994; Roche, 1995; Fox Harding, 1997; Franklin, 2002).

Children's rights

As Hill and Tisdall (1997) and others have pointed out, the new sociology of childhood is naturally sympathetic towards the promotion of children's rights, particularly participatory rights. However, rights come in various forms and with various implications. For this reason, debate on children's rights is frequently contentious not only with respect to the content of such 'rights' – for example, the relative importance of rights to protection, economic security, involvement and participation – but also to the extent to which a focus on the latter form of rights threatens family relationships. Indeed, the recent history of claims in relation to children's rights is closely connected with the deconstruction of functionalist and consensual notions of the family and with changing conceptions of adulthood and childhood. In short:

> In the latter decades of the twentieth century, adult lives became more flexible, and adulthood became less stable and less complete. As flexibility enters adult life in our age of uncertainty, it is becoming harder to see children and adults as opposites. It is becoming increasingly difficult to justify forms of adult authority over children that depend on the clear distinction between adult and child (Lee, 2001, p. 21).

Whilst some analysts of childhood would see positives in such uncertainty (for example, Wyness, 2000), the 'crisis in childhood' can be easily translated, for adults, into a crisis of authority and control. The 1989 United Nations Convention on the Rights of the Child (UNCRC) was both a reflection of and also encouraged such uncertainty and concern.

Although the League of Nations had produced a declaration of children's rights as long ago as 1924, the rights it advocated were largely rights to protection. Its five brief principles focus chiefly on welfare; the means for normal development, food and medicine, relief in times of distress, protection against exploitation and social-isation to serve others. The UN itself produced a Declaration of the Rights of the Child in 1959. Its ten principles broadly echoed the rights of the 1924 declaration in its focus on protection and welfare. Although there was a focus on the healthy and well-rounded development of children, there was no specific encouragement in relation to involvement and participation in decision-making. The UN Convention (ratified by the UK in 1991), which replaced the 1959 Declaration, argued for a more participatory view of rights. While most of its substantive articles, such as Articles 2, 3 and 6, echoed the themes of the 1959 declaration, other articles added a new dimension. Article 12 requires State Parties to:

> Assure to the child who is capable of forming his or her own views the right to express these views freely in all matters affecting the child, the views of the child being given due weight in accordance with the age and maturity of the child (quoted in Freeman, 2002, p. 100).

Further articles in the Convention both reinforce and substantiate the position of Article 12: Article 13, the right to 'freedom of expression'; Article 14, the right to 'freedom of thought, conscience and religion'; Article 15, the right to 'freedom of association'; Article 16, the right to 'privacy'; and Article 17, the right to information through the mass media and other sources (for example, children's books).

As well as reflecting uncertainty over family relationships, this development of interest in children's rights to participation in the latter decades of the twentieth century is also consistent with the growth of uncertainty and doubt with respect to many of the virtues of modernity, the State and state welfare systems. In the UK, this uncertainty was reflected in the 1989 Children Act, which sought to both limit the role of the state with respect to parents and also enhance the rights and involvement of children. The latter is evident with respect to a wide variety of contexts:

- Statutory social services complaints procedures for young people.
- An expanded right to separate legal representation; that is, separate from parents.

- The right to refuse medical or psychiatric assessment; subject to the child being judged to be 'of sufficient understanding'.
- The right to initiate legal proceedings, subject to judicial discretion.
- Recommendations on 'involvement' in the Act's regulations and guidance.

However, despite UK ratification of the UNCRC, neither Conservatives nor New Labour have exhibited wholehearted commitment to involvement and participation (Lansdown, 2001). Indeed, the UK government has been heavily criticised by the United Nations Committee on the Rights of the Child in its 2002 overview of the UK's progress in implementing the Convention (Featherstone et al., 2002). In relation to children and young people, the UK government has parcelled out 'rights' where it deems them appropriate (for example, in relation to looked after children) and has focused on 'responsibilities' in other areas affecting children and young people (such as youth justice).

Alongside the UNCRC and the 1989 Children Act, the third major development to have significant implications for children's rights in the UK has been the passing of the Human Rights Act in 1998. This became fully operational in October 2000 and incorporates the European Convention on Human Rights (ECHR) into UK law. Since there are no age limits, the Act can clearly apply to children. However, Fortin (2002a,b), whilst seeing considerable future potential for the Act, identifies two problems that currently stand in the way of significant use of the Act by children and which make its implications for children's rights ambiguous. The first of these is that Strasbourg has traditionally taken a cautious approach to the concept of children having rights as individuals, separate from their parents. The second limitation is that there is a relative lack of case law on children's rights thus far. To some extent, this stems from the Convention's focus on civil and political rights – which reflects its origins in the aftermath of the Second World War. Moreover, rights such as the right to a 'private and family life' are potentially more favourable to parents than children (Herring, 2001).

Conclusion

This chapter has reviewed a range of contemporary developments in thinking about children which seek to locate children as beings rather than becomings and to advance 'rights' claims for them as persons. This is helpful in assessing contemporary child welfare policy. For example, the attempt to reduce child poverty, imbued with notions of investment, is nevertheless also a praiseworthy attempt to improve children's lives in the present. On the other hand, it is rarely justified as such; in this context, as in others, the investment rationale prevails. Some of the measures being promoted, such as the desirability of parental involvement in paid work, have problematic features and may actively militate against improving quality of life in the present for both parents and children (see Chapter 3).

However, the overall picture is quite complex and mixed. For example, there is a considerable recent emphasis on investing in early years provision (see Pugh, 2003) but little emphasis on consulting with children about such initiatives. In contrast, the establishment of a Children and Young Person's Unit in 2000 which took responsibility for administering the Children's Fund, a fund for children aged 4–13, places emphasis on consulting with children and young people and has put efforts into imaginative consultation processes and to developing local panels of young people to comment on services. The difference can be partly explained in terms of assumptions that younger children cannot be meaningfully consulted with but may also reflect differing approaches by differing parts of the state and associated experts. For example, early years provision is strongly influenced by the discipline of developmental psychology. Whatever impetus there is towards consultation is in relation to specific strategies or services rather than in relation to child welfare more generally.

CHAPTER 3

Family Policy

The main part of our family policy is about ensuring that children are better supported, everything springs from that (Home Office spokesperson quoted in *The Guardian*, 27 March 2000).

An important, if not the dominant, tendency in relation to contemporary family policy is that the welfare of children, rather than that of adults, provides the central rationale. In this chapter, we explore the main contours of the policies and activities which have emerged in this field and which stem from this rationale. We locate this analysis within a brief overview of dominant approaches to family policy in the twentieth century and chart the continuities and discontinuities under New Labour.

What is family policy?

The concept of family policy is problematic and frequently confusing (Fox Harding, 1996). It conjures up a picture of a policy with coherent and clear objectives, identifiable assumptions and predictable effects. Lister (2000) notes the dangers of assuming that there is something called the state which acts in a unified way to develop family policy. In practice, there are usually a range of policies emanating from a range of sources which may conflict with one another. It is also a policy area that is particularly prone to the use of rhetoric on the part of governments. This has often meant that what is said is quite different to what is done, although of course that does not mean that rhetoric does not in itself perform particular purposes. For example, rhetoric by governments in relation to family can act to construct certain kinds of families as legitimate and others as not (Fairclough, 2000; Driver and Martell, 2002).

Historically, the UK has been considered to either not have a national family policy at all or, at the most, to have implicit family policies (Wassof and Dey, 2000). Implicit family policies are government actions and policies not specifically or primarily addressed to the family, but which have indirect consequences (Kamerman and Kahn, 1978, p. 3).

However, there have been particular assumptions underpinning successive government approaches. First, at the beginning of the welfare state the model of the family underpinning the tax and benefit systems was that of the male breadwinner supporting a dependent wife and children. Indeed, the Beveridge Report which laid the foundations of the modern welfare state has been strongly criticised, particularly by feminists, for the primacy attached to the male breadwinner model (for example, see Pascall, 1986; Lister, 1994). As Skevik (2003, p. 427) notes, however, children's allowances were a key element of Beveridge's framework without which he judged his proposals unsustainable. This leads her to pose an important question: did this emphasis on children's allowances mark a break away from the overall focus on supporting breadwinners and point towards a genuine recognition of children as claimants? She argues, however, that Beveridge saw children's allowances as a means of resolving problems in the adult world: 'Children's allowances should be paid to families not because children had a right to benefit, but because children implied expenses to the family' (p. 427). Alongside this key argument were concerns about the low birth rate and the quality of children for the future. As Skevik among others have noted (see Hendrick, 1994, 2003; Daniel and Ivatts, 1998), Beveridge was concerned with children as an investment for the future, although it is important to note that, children's allowances aside, they were neglected in terms of further specific post-war policy initiatives (see Chapter 4 for further discussion).

Although normatively accepted, the male breadwinner model was one to which many families did not or could not conform in the post-war decades. As Land (1999) notes, with the eventual return to pre-Second World War deregulated and flexible labour markets, the numbers of men without a wage, let alone a family wage, rose. From 1979, when the Conservatives came to power, until 1997, the number of children living in households where there was no one in employment doubled. Two-thirds of lone-parent families and one in twelve two-parent families were dependent upon income support in 1997. Land argues that the increase in uptake of family credit and its predecessor, family income support supplement, illustrated the difficulties of supporting a family on one wage. A key development of course was the introduction of child benefit in 1977 – the only benefit that was and is payable in respect of all children regardless of parental income or labour market status.

Secondly, a key assumption of UK governments has been that raising children is in the main a responsibility to be undertaken by families. Whilst educating children is an activity to be undertaken by government, their care is not a proper concern of governments except when things go wrong. According to Daniel and Ivatts, this was an important underlying principle of the post-1945 Beveridge model of welfare and central to the philosophy of the Conservatives. They further argue that this is now reflected in the social policy values espoused by New Labour, although we will contest this in our subsequent discussion (Daniel and Ivatts, 1998). This view – that the child is primarily the responsibility of individual parents – has posed long-standing dilemmas for the state. For example, Frost and Stein (1989) note the difficulties of state institutions attempting to influence families while ensuring that such families maintain their private character (see also Donzelot, 1980; Parton, 1991).

The centrality of notions of individual family responsibility and associated concerns about family privacy has meant, for example, that developments in the UK have been in strong contrast to a country such as Sweden, where a social democratic understanding of the relationship between family and state has resulted in a system where the 'provision, socialization and care of children are regarded as responsibilities to be shared between parents and the welfare state, supported by employers' (Björnberg, 2002, p. 36). However, in the UK a residualist approach to services has developed. This approach has legitimated intervention primarily for those who are defined as problematic (although the boundaries of what is considered problematic have varied historically). It has also meant that notions of family responsibility have assumed and, in practice, reinforced women's responsibility for the welfare of children. As indicated, whilst education was provided on a universal basis to children, responsibility for their care rested with parents, leading to the splitting of their care and education, a split which has been increasingly contested. Developments under New Labour (discussed below) have rendered this split less rigid than hitherto.

The election of a New Labour government in the UK in 1997 altered the policy context after years of New Right dominance. This has led to a complex picture in terms of how and where the balance between responsibilities is to be struck. Before examining this it is useful to explore the Conservative years as they have profoundly influenced, as well as formed an important backdrop for, contemporary developments.

Pre-1997 – pre-modern panics

Despite some strong rhetoric and the presence of a diverse constituency of pro-family values pressure groups, the Thatcher years do not present a picture of a Conservatism that was centrally concerned with the family and traditional values. The picture under the Major governments was even more mixed (Fox Harding, 1999; Somerville, 2000). However, at particular points there was evidence of a considerable level of moral posturing and legislative action in relation to specific groups, such as lone mothers (Mann and Roseneil, 1999; Skinner, 2003). Under the Major governments, there were cuts in lone-parent benefit.

Another development which illustrated Conservative support for traditional family values was the passage of Section 28 of the Local Government Act 1988. This measure, which prohibited the promotion of homosexuality by local authorities, was argued by some commentators to be the greatest success of the pro-family values campaigners (Fox Harding, 1996). However, divorce became easier and the disadvantages of illegitimacy were reduced. The Thatcher government took a clearly oppositional stance on the family values approach of Victoria Gillick, who unsuccessfully undertook legal action designed to ensure that children under the age of 16 could not be given contraceptive treatment or advice without parental consent.

A key legislative measure produced by the Conservatives was the Child Support Act 1991. This obliged non-residential parents, primarily fathers, to be financially responsible for their children. The measure was targeted mainly at those on state benefits and was clearly designed to reduce welfare expenditure. However, it also fed into wider concerns about parental responsibility (Williams, 1998). Other legislation introduced under the Conservatives, such as the Children Act 1989, the Criminal Justice Act 1991 and the Criminal Justice and Public Order Act 1994, emphasised parental responsibility as lifelong, binding and determined by biology (Fox Harding, 1999). In the field of divorce, the uncoupling of marriage and parenthood meant that the idea of divorce as a clean break, primarily between fathers and their children, was superseded by a policy presumption that prioritised parenthood over spousal obligations (Smart and Neale, 1999). Overall, under the Conservatives there was a preparedness to expand parents' responsibilities for children, but little consistency existed in the support offered to parents (Fox Harding, 1999). European Union initiatives to improve parental leave were blocked and calls to develop a National Childcare Strategy were ignored (Skinner, 2003).

According to Fox Harding (1999), there was a conflict within Conservatism between economic liberals and traditional authoritarian conservatives. Whereas much of the ideology of the right emphasised a restricted role for the state, family values campaigners sought more prescription and legislation. Equally, the emphasis of economic liberals on individual autonomy and the unfettered right of the market to dictate all forms of relationships clashed with that of the traditional authoritarians, who espoused a strong state, commitment to nationhood, law and order and the policing of behaviour. Such divides militated against a clear consensus on family issues and policies, although in practice there was some accommodation of the conflicting ideologies. 'Libertarian Conservatism', adopted by the New Right in Britain and the US, supported laissez-faire economics and a strong state to maintain traditional and family values. However, this accommodation was uneasy when applied to some issues. For example, there were tensions over whether the mothers of young children should be in paid work and whether employers should take any account of workers' family commitments. Therefore, whilst the Conservatives presided over an historically unprecedented increase in women, including mothers of young children, entering paid work, their record on supporting publicly provided child care generally was poor. The 1990s saw the emergence of accounts from working mothers which highlighted the consequences for everyday family life (Freely, 1996; Benn, 1998). Such accounts documented the amount of juggling required to sustain work and home and led Benn to argue that working mothers inhabited two worlds whose priorities clashed – the world of work and home. Moreover, her research demonstrated the plight of mothers, lone or otherwise, who wished to work but could not find work which was adequately remunerated and, in particular, could not meet the costs of the child care required.

Overall, there were considerable changes in family life, particularly in relation to family form, which coincided to some extent but not completely with Conservative rule from 1979 to 1997 (see Frost and

Featherstone, 2003). Reliance on statistics here can mask complex social realities. For example, lone-parent households with dependent children increased from 2 per cent of the total in 1961 to 7 per cent of the total by 1998–1999. However, they need to be located in the context of a growth in cohabitation and a decline in 'shotgun' marriages. Whilst births outside marriage rose steadily throughout the 1970s, 1980s and 1990s, reaching about 38 per cent of all live births in 1998, the vast majority of births are jointly registered. The statistics on single, never married women, including mothers, are misleading. While a woman may cohabit and have a child who is jointly registered, if the adults separate the mother will appear in the statistics as single rather than separated. Furthermore, since the number of shotgun marriages following a pregnancy has declined, such a pregnancy is now most likely to lead to cohabitation; with the mothers registered as single if the cohabitation breaks down. The rise in divorce rates throughout the 1970s and 1980s also needs to be located to some extent in an understanding of the impact of legislative changes in the early 1970s, stemming from the Divorce Reform Act of 1969, for those awaiting divorces, and it is important to note that rates started to level off in the mid-1990s.

Notwithstanding such qualifications, throughout the period of Conservative rule divorce rates were the highest in Europe and there was a considerable increase in lone motherhood. There was also a considerable increase in cohabitation rates and in the numbers of children born outside marriage (see Somerville, 2000, for a discussion of the continuities and discontinuities of marital and fertility patterns, particularly post-war; also, Frost and Featherstone, 2003). Also, as we have already noted in Chapter 1, there was a dramatic increase in child poverty which was unique to the UK among Western industrial countries (Bradshaw, 2002, 2003; Skinner, 2003).

What has happened under New Labour?

The post-war settlement was based upon particular assumptions about the desirability of full male employment, of families based upon a division between male breadwinner and homemaker wife, and a nation based on the legacy of an imperial past and particular conceptions of race (Newman, 2001; see also Williams, 1989). However, as indicated, such assumptions did not mean that coherent policies were always pursued (Land, 1999). Furthermore, it became increasingly clear in the 1990s that this post-war settlement had been profoundly fractured at a range of levels. There are a range of analyses of how and why New Labour developed specific responses to such fracturing (for example see Giddens, 1998; Newman, 2001). As Newman states, New Labour should be understood as an unstable project which attempts to engage a range of diverse and, indeed, often contradictory constituencies. Certainly, in relation to family policy a range of diverse constituencies have been mobilised and appealed to (see Driver and Martell, 2002). The subsequent trajectory has been uneven and inconsistent, as we shall see, for example, in relation to an early espousal of marriage as the best form in which to bring up children (see Skinner, 2003 and discussion below).

When, in the early 1990s, New Labour was formulating its political identity generally, it engaged in a rethinking of 'Old' Labour ideas as well as articulating its critique of New Right approaches. In terms of family policy, Driver and Martell argue that they saw Thatcherites as economic individualists whose only concern was the free market – an approach which was seen as destructive of forms of community such as the family. However, they also challenged what they saw as the social individualism of Old Labour. It 'was too focused on rights-claiming at the expense of individual and collective responsibilities; and it stood back non-judgementally from a range of social problems where government intervention is now thought to be required' (Driver and Martell, 2002, p. 202). Whilst these caricatures distort the diversity and complexity of post-war politics, they served New Labour well and fitted with the concerns of key social moralists such as Tony Blair (see Rentoul, 2001). Furthermore, Hendrick (2003) argues that a key event in the early 1990s, the murder of the child James Bulger by two other children, was pivotal. It confirmed a deep-rooted pessimism in adults about children and reinforced the need for action against urban deprivation. He argues that it is important to note its coincidence with the period when New Labour was articulating its political identity.

Crucially, we would add that it also fed into concerns that something needed to be done about the perceived linkages between children's involvement in criminality, changes in family form and parental behaviour. This is not to say that there was or indeed is consensus about why or what should be done. For example, as Driver and Martell (2002, p. 203) note, there are considerable differences between Tony Blair and academics such as Anthony Giddens, who has been strongly associated with the New Labour project.

Giddens and Blair have a different view on individualism and therefore to some extent what should be promoted in relation to family policy. Giddens sees growing individualism not, as Blair seems to, as a product of economic egoism that needs to be counteracted by more community. Rather it is a symptom of post-traditional modernisation, where people have more choice, reflexivity and control – developments which are to be celebrated.

Whilst Blair lays stronger emphasis on the two-parent family and on the family as the basis for stability in society, Driver and Martell argue that 'Rather than aspiring to a traditional family that can offer stability and security in a fast moving world, Giddens argues that the family should be seen as part of that world, expressing flexibility and change instead of acting as a counterbalance to them' (Giddens, 1998; Driver and Martell, 2002, p. 204; see also Frost and Featherstone, 2003).

In practice, we see an accommodation between these two strands, with an apparent consensus that what is of ultimate importance is the welfare of children. Thus, whilst apparently espousing flexibility, Giddens (1998) then comes up with pretty rigid policy approaches such as parenting contracts, which reinforce that parenthood is lifelong even if adult relationships are not and, whilst the government have not introduced such contracts, they have certainly continued the trends in this direction which emerged under the Conservatives.

It is important to note that what appeared to preoccupy New Labour in opposition or in the early years of government has shifted in some respects over the years. Skinner (2003) notes one particular shift. The pledge by Tony Blair to abolish child poverty has 'driven a clearer more focused rhetoric which has moved away from strengthening families and marriage *per se* to one more firmly embedded in improving the life chances and opportunities for children' (Skinner, 2003, p. 23). However, alongside this has been a consistent focus on emphasising and enforcing parents' responsibilities towards their children and intervening to change their behaviour.

In the next sections, we outline what has happened in relation to these emphases. We start by looking at what Skinner describes as two distinct perspectives of the family policy agenda: general support for families with children; and specific initiatives for supporting poor families. These not only overlap but are linked in that more general policies should help stop more families falling into poverty, and policies targeted at poor families help to lift them out of poverty.

Supporting families

There have been a number of initiatives in terms of general support for families. For example, the value of Child Benefit has been increased. Also, a National ChildCare Strategy, which aimed to improve the availability, affordability and quality of child care, was announced in the 1998 Consultation Document: *Meeting the ChildCare Challenge*. There has also been an increase in maternity leave, the introduction for the first time of 2 weeks' paternity leave and of 3 months' unpaid parental leave. Alongside this, parents of children under 5 or with a disability have been given the right to request flexible working arrangements.

These are universal approaches designed for all those with children. In terms of support for poor families with children, the key elements of such policies are 'to minimise the risks of some aspects of social exclusion, such as alleviating financial poverty through improving social security benefits for children, but also by promoting independence through employment, through neighbourhood regeneration, and through specific programmes aimed at poor families to provide general health and welfare support in a mixed economy of care' (Skinner, 2003, p. 27). Skinner identifies three key strategies: financial support for poor families; welfare to work strategies; and targeted support for poor/disadvantaged children.

Income support has been uprated but not to a level likely to meet the needs of families to the full. The dominant strategy has been to 'make work pay' through tax credits; such as the Working Tax Credit, which is paid to all employed adults on low earnings whether they have children or not. However, the amount is higher for those with children. The ChildCare Tax Credit is available for child care costs and the Child Tax Credit is available to all with children, whether working or not, although employment status will have a bearing on the level of the credit. Alongside substantial changes in the benefit system largely, but not exclusively, designed to make work pay, programmes targeted at specific groups have been developed. Five groups were targeted under the New Deal Programme: lone parents, young people, long-term unemployed people, disabled people, partners of unemployed people, and unemployed people over the age of 50. Initially, participation in the New Deal was voluntary for lone parents but over time they have been required to attend work-focused interviews when their youngest child reached school age, with failure to do so possibly resulting in benefit reduction. Finally, in terms of targeted support for poor/disadvantaged children there have been a plethora of initiatives.

Skinner notes that 2 years after *Supporting Families: A Consultation Document* (Home Office, 1998c) was published (according to the foreword by Jack Straw, then Home Secretary, the first government consultation document on family policy published by a British government), there was a shift in emphasis from focusing on families to focusing on children, noting the importance, for example, of the establishment of a Children and Young Person's Unit in November 2000. Central to this have been targeted initiatives in relation to either poor children or children living in poor areas. Particular stages of children's lives have been singled out for particular attention, reflecting what has become a consensus that prevention in early years is key. Thus, there has been an unprecedented level of resources devoted to early years support (Pugh, 2003, p. 186). Initiatives here include: governmental restructuring; increased expenditure on nursery education; the introduction of Early Years Development and ChildCare Partnerships in local authorities; the establishment of the Early Excellence Centres, pilot programmes followed by neighbourhood nurseries and children's centres; 522 Sure Start programmes in deprived areas; establishment of the foundation stage of early education for children; the production of a national qualifications and training framework for the early years; and an integrated inspection service.

For children over the age of 4, there is the Children's Fund, which was, until governmental restructuring, run by the Children and Young Person's Unit. This funding stream is available to all local authorities and is therefore universal. However, its priorities are focused on the prevention of early difficulties such as truancy, offending and anti-social behaviour (see Jeffery, 2003). Finally, the Connexions service offers advice, support and guidance to help young people aged 13–19 in the transition to adulthood and is designed to ensure that they continue on into training, learning or paid work (Garrett, 2002).

An important development in relation to services has been the integration of the education and care of children in one government department, the Department for Education and Skills (DfES). In 2003, most children's services in relation to care, protection and education were located in this department and a minister for Children and Young People was appointed for the first time. A Cabinet Committee for Children and Young People, set up in July 2000, and the Children and Young Person's Unit have also been integrated into this department.

Discussion

To recap briefly on arguments rehearsed in Chapter 1, the key elements of a discourse around social investment are premised upon a belief that whilst the old welfare state sought to protect people from the market, a social investment state seeks to facilitate the integration of people into the market. People's security therefore comes from their capacity to change; thus the emphasis on investing in human capital and lifelong learning as the surest form of security.

The notion is that such investments will be more suited to the labour markets of global capitalism, in which job security is rare, and flexibility is highly valued. For its part, social policy should be 'productivist' and investment oriented, rather than distributive and consumption oriented. The emphasis in social policy should shift from consumption and income maintenance programs to those that invest in people and enhance their capacity to participate in the productive economy (Jenson and Saint-Martin, 2001, p. 5; Lister, 2003).

This builds on a discourse from economics which has promoted constructions of people, crucially children, as wealth that can be augmented by investment. For state spending to be effective and worthwhile, it must not be simply consumed in the present but must be an investment that will pay off and reap rewards in the future. Thus, spending may legitimately be directed to: supporting and educating children because they hold the promise of the future; to promoting health and healthy populations because they pay off in future lower costs; to reducing the probability of future costs of school failure and crime with a heavy emphasis on children and to fostering employability so as to increase future labour force participation rates.

Spending on current needs, by contrast, needs to be cautious and targeted and is motivated not just by reasons of social justice but also to reduce the threat to social cohesion posed by those who are marginalised. Inclusion of the marginalised is a necessary current expenditure. A key theme then is the importance of investing in children as they embody the future and in the process an instrumental approach to children is promoted. Furthermore, adults become constructed not in their own right but only insofar as they facilitate the project of investing in children. The social investment thesis goes a considerable way to explaining much of the above. In particular, initiatives such as Sure Start seem highly compatible, with their focus on early years, although it is also important to note the prioritisation of employability issues and the prevention of criminality in other developments such as the Children's Fund and Connexions. Given the focus on children what are the implications for their parents?

Reordering adults?

New Labour has intervened in complex and not always consistent ways in developments and debates about family form and has continued to expand constructions of parents' responsibilities. In their consultation document *Supporting Families* (Home Office, 1998c), it was argued that children were best raised in a family form comprising a married couple and they set out a number of initiatives to support marriage. These have continued, funded by the Lord Chancellor's Department (National Family and Parenting Institute, 2002, hereafter referred to as the NFPI). An Advisory Group on Marriage and Relationship Support was established by the Lord Chancellor, with a remit to develop a co-ordinated and proactive strategy for marriage and relationship support and to assess the impact of government measures intended to prevent relationship breakdown. However, statements in Supporting Families exemplified the high point of a commitment to marriage and a range of developments have ensued which either water down or contradict this commitment (Skinner, 2003). Part II of the 1996 Family Law Act, which aimed to save marriages, has been repealed and the married couples tax allowance abolished. No policies on marriage were outlined in the Labour Party Manifesto for 2001. Parental responsibility is to be extended to unmarried fathers who register the child's birth and, in its second term, the government has included both same sex and cohabiting couples as adopters in adoption legislation. It is planned to develop legislation offering same sex couples access to legal and financial rights in order that they might have a degree of parity with heterosexual married couples. Interestingly, heterosexual cohabitees will not be offered the same opportunities.

There has been ongoing support for a range of initiatives aimed at lessening the impact of relationship breakdown on children: the launch of a Parenting Plan for Divorcing and Separating Parents in 2002 by the Lord Chancellor's Department; the launch of a website funded by the Lord Chancellor's Department by the National Children's Bureau, designed to give online support and information for children whose parents are divorcing or separating; and a long-term strategy to provide a national network of child contact centres which can provide a safe and neutral venue for non-resident parents and their children to maintain contact (NFPI, 2002).

It is clear that New Labour has in the main adopted a pragmatic approach to family form, although in its treatment of heterosexual cohabitees it could be argued that it has fallen well short of recognising and legally supporting flexibility in how people choose to live family life. Generally, however, we would concur with Lewis that New Labour's main preoccupation has not been 'the unity of the couple, or even the permanence of relationships, but the need to secure stable arrangements for children' (Lewis, 2001, p. 178). Therefore, there is a continuation of trends towards constructing parenthood as lifelong even if marital relationships do not endure. This of course is a reordering project in that it does not allow adult men and women to have a clean break. A key and also constant feature has been a continued focus on the responsibilities of *parents*.

Parents and their responsibilities

As Lister (2003) notes, in return for the promise of investment in economic opportunity by the state, increased emphasis is being placed upon the responsibilities of citizens in a number of respects: to equip themselves to respond to the challenges of economic globalisation through improved employability; to support themselves through paid work; to invest in their own pensions; and to accept responsibility for their children. This latter responsibility found expression in key pieces of legislation under the Conservatives, such as the Child Support Act 1991 and the Children Act 1989, and has been continued and expanded under New Labour and has been inserted into its broader project.

The considerable amount of governmental activity in relation to parenting has resulted in a diverse array of workers across a range of practice sites (see Henricson *et al.*, 2001, for a discussion about the diverse constituencies and agendas involved). Many of the initiatives are predicated on parents changing their own behaviour; for example, to find paid work, to become more involved with their children, and to supervise their children more effectively. An example of an initiative which requires parents to change their own behaviour on the assumption that this will lead to better outcomes for children is Sure Start (Waldfogel, 1997; Jeffery, 2003). Such changes can

encompass the cessation of smoking during pregnancy and involvement in paid work. The introduction of parenting orders under the
Crime and Disorder Act (1998) is an example of an initiative which
requires parents to change both their and their children's behaviour.

Targeted, if poorly funded and time limited, initiatives directed
at parents have emerged under the Family Support Grant. This
funding stream, based at the Home Office until 2003, supported both
new and established services on the basis of themes set annually. Such
themes have included work with fathers, minority ethnic parents and
disabled parents. These themes are based on the assumptions that
such parents are hard to reach and/or need extra support.

Parents' responsibilities have been reconstructed. For example,
gone is the option of full-time parenting except for those who can
afford it (Land, 1999). Mothers are now expected to behave like
fathers; that is, as workers in a universal breadwinner model of
welfare. Indeed, for many proponents of the social investment
thesis, such as Esping-Andersen (2002), women's involvement in the
paid labour force is central to tackling child poverty. Whilst this may
be in tune with many women's own desires, it raises considerable concerns for those who point to gendered inequalities in the labour
market and the continuing inadequacy of the support infrastructure
(McRobbie, 2000; see discussion below). It is also argued that attempts
to impose the prioritisation of work over caring responsibilities are out
of tune with how many women wish to order their responsibilities. The
labour dispute at Heathrow Airport in the summer of 2003 highlights
that, for many women, caring responsibilities and institutional
flexibility, in order to discharge such responsibilities, are crucial.

Williams (1998) has argued that the language around parenting
and parental responsibility holds considerable dangers for women
in that it obscures what would appear to be happening in terms of
material practices. It treats gender equality as a given rather than a
goal. From the evaluation of the parenting programmes delivered
under the Crime and Disorder Act (1998), it would appear that it is
largely women who are involved as participants, whether on a
voluntary or compulsory basis, on programmes which reinforce
their responsibility for their sons' behaviour. Ghate and Ramalla
(2002) found that 81 per cent of those who attended were women
and half were lone parents. They reported very high levels of need,
ranging from problems of debt to health and relationship problems
and more than eight in ten said that they particularly wanted help
in managing a difficult child. Moreover, the overwhelming majority
of children and young people who were the source of concern
were male.

There are, as was indicated above, small, time-limited streams of funding emanating from the Home Office which are offering specific grants to work with 'fathers' and a national organisation, Fathers Direct, has been supported. To some extent, as Scourfield and Drakeford (2002) argue, New Labour is making 'masculinity policy' in its appeals to men as fathers in some arenas. The Conservatives, via the Child Support Act 1991, targeted absent parents, which in practice meant fathers, but this was not accompanied by any attempts to either insist on fathers' physical presence or that they offer an emotional and child care contribution. Indeed, the primary motivation seemed to be to reduce welfare expenditure rather than increase economic resources to women and children.

New Labour has introduced 2 weeks' paid paternity leave at the birth of a child, which has been described as a 'small symbolic step' (O'Sullivan, 2001). Whilst an improvement on what was there before, it does little to tackle entrenched and general gendered patterns in relation to the labour market or caretaking. Particular groups of fathers have been targeted for particular funding initiatives – those who are young and/or unemployed. The rationale for such initiatives can be located in discourses which emerged in the 1990s which identify such men as particularly feckless/problematic (Williams, 1998). The 'official' rationale offered in *Supporting Families: A Consultation Document* is that father involvement benefits sons. This rationale stems from a discourse which subscribes to a complex variety of insights into fatherhood from sex role theory and social learning theory, the evidence for which is disputed by many researchers (Lamb, 1997). There has been little effort to position initiatives within discourses which stress the importance of gender equity, or to offer broad supports to all men to share care.

It is important to note that elements of an agenda which seeks to restructure relationships between men and women in equitable ways are apparent in a range of initiatives which have emerged in relation to domestic violence, even though these are usually promoted in gender-neutral language. Initiatives include commitments to develop a helpline, to improve the resourcing of refuges, and to improve reporting and court practices. However, initiatives in relation to domestic violence are being pursued in isolation from those directed at engaging fathers, which can lead to tensions in practice, and there is little evidence of joint-up thinking here (Featherstone, 2003). An important note to be made here, in summary, is that while women are being encouraged to become workers, men are not receiving the kind of support necessary to become carers. This is explored further below.

Are things getting better then?

Chapter 1 documented the gains that have been made in tackling children's poverty, gains which are important and to be applauded. However, the reliance on involvement in paid work as a central means of tackling such poverty has considerable implications for both children and parents at a number of levels. Toynbee (2003) vividly documents the realities of working in a low-waged casualised economy from her own personal experience as an adult. There is growing evidence of the difficulties posed by a casualised economy, where many parents, men and women work 'atypical' (defined as evenings and weekends) hours, and of the implications that this has for their caring responsibilities (Dean, 2002). When asked, children have expressed considerable antipathy to their parents working on either evenings or weekends (Ghazi, 2003).

Furthermore, Toynbee (2003, p. 233) graphically illustrates how low pay continues to be an urgent issue, particularly for women who are usually mothers. Low-paid women always were and still are in largely segregated work, doing the traditional three Cs – catering, cleaning and caring. Seventy per cent of the low-paid are still women. She points out that the minimum wage introduced by New Labour has been set at too low a level and provides compelling evidence from her own experience of the difficulties the low-paid are currently experiencing. 'I have been shocked to find that many pay-rates in the bottom jobs are much the same or mainly lower in real terms than thirty years ago, tangible proof of how the low-paid have been left behind' (p. 228).

She also raises the issue of child care, noting how often the lack of child care forces women to stay in low paid jobs which they can organise around their child care responsibilities. According to Lister (2003), the aim of developing a National ChildCare Strategy represents the first time a government has accepted that child care is a public as well as a private responsibility, and marks a significant shift from post-war developments in relation to the welfare state. However, the initial welcome extended to the commitment has not lasted. The reliance on the private, for-profit sector to supply much of the child care provision has been questioned (Land, 2002). Other related concerns have been raised about the cost of child care, the inadequacy of government financial supports in the face of such costs and the geographical gaps in provision (Pacey, 2002; Roberts, 2003). Despite ongoing calls for universal child care provision funded by governments and the evidence that this would have a variety of benefits for parents and children, including aiding the tackling of child poverty (Pacey, 2002), targeting continues to be a strong feature of government provision. Proposals in relation to parental leave have been considered timid and are situated within an overriding concern with what the business community would find acceptable (Lister, 2003).

There has been more targeted support for poor families, as was outlined above, and there has been a complex reordering of the welfare system to 'provide a continuing stream of income for families with children, irrespective of whether the adults in the family are in work, and which can be relied on by families who move into work; to pay support for children to the main carer, in line with Child Benefit; to remove the stigma attached to claiming the traditional forms of support for the poorest families, by creating one system of income-related support for all families with children; and to enable families to access financial support from one system, even as their income rises or circumstances change' (Skinner, 2003, p. 30). Given that some of the changes came into operation only in April 2003, it will take time to assess their impact. They have the potential to remove stigma, and payment to the main carer is designed to ensure maximum benefit for children. However, developments such as the Working Families Tax Credit, which has been Gordon Brown's chief method of lifting children out of poverty, are complex and difficult to calculate by individuals. Moreover, there is a problem with reliance on targeted measures in that many who are eligible do not claim. For example, Toynbee notes research indicating that many more poor families fail to claim than actually receive the credits.

A broader critique of the apparent privileging of paid work over caring responsibilities comes from a diverse range of writers who focus on what is often referred to as the 'ethic of care' (see Williams, 1999, 2001). This critique poses a significant challenge to the values underpinning the social investment state and draws attention to the complexity and fluidity attached to the relationships between carers and receivers. This has particular resonance for rethinking identities such as 'parent' or 'child'. The ethic of care starts from the recognition that we all give and receive care as part of the interdependence of the human condition and rejects the normative and gendered assumption that the human developmental path is away from dependence towards independence. Policies should therefore be developed around the giving and receiving of care as a fundamental, universal activity, rather than paid work being seen as the pre-eminent activity around which the giving and receiving of care is organised. This could involve a reconstruction of parenting identities, particularly if tied to a project on gendered change as well as a rethinking of notions of dependency when attached to children.

As Williams notes, writings from within this perspective pose a considerable challenge to the values underpinning contemporary policies. Whilst not addressing this perspective, Toynbee makes compatible points about what she sees as distorted societal priorities which construct a wage structure which places essential work such as caring at the bottom.

A key concern is that an instrumental approach to children is readily apparent in particular policy emphases. For example, there is a considerable emphasis on early years initiatives, which can contribute to two worrying tendencies. Older children's concerns may be less well attended to and an instrumental approach can mean the investment is not continued if there is not seen to be a clear pay off (Lister, 2003). As worryingly, if children do not turn out as desired, they may be even more criminalised and demonised than older children are currently (see Chapter 6). The positioning of the majority of services for children within the DfES can be read as an attempt to tie policy and practices with children very narrowly into an instrumental project, although it does have the potential also to integrate services which have been split in problematic ways since the Second World War.

An under-addressed question is how well, if at all, does the notion of 'investment' concur with how children see themselves and how parents see their children. A small example in relation to the former would support suggestions that children are as concerned with their present as their future. For example, Draper (2001) documents how, when asked about the provision offered by their early years centre, children were most concerned about the number and quality of friends they made at the centre; and, indeed, that was a concern of their parents too, a concern which was not reflected in the myriad of measuring instruments used to monitor the effectiveness of the centre.

As was outlined in Chapter 2, the meanings attached to children by adults are shifting and often relate quite strongly to shifting experiences of unstable adult relationships. Children variously signify emotional connectedness, belonging and are often the repository of expressive values signifying an escape from the instrumentality of the 'public' world of work and achievement. Consequently, there are important questions to be asked about the degree of disjuncture there can be between constructions of children as investments in policy developments and parents' own understandings.

A key issue which was hinted at in Draper's article and does emerge from our experiences of evaluating Sure Start initiatives is the importance of not assuming that government policies translate seamlessly into implementation. Our experience is that in initiatives such as Sure Start workers have to mediate between the needs of those they work with and their paymasters if their programmes are to be invested in by those they seek to engage. If parents do not see the point of smoking-cessation programmes, they will simply not come. Less starkly, they will pick and choose between aspects of programmes.

A final observation is that whilst programmes such as Sure Start may be premised upon notions of children as investment, this does not mean that children may not experience considerable improvements in the quality of life in the here and now. Government ministers may be focused on the future, very often grandiosely – 'Support for today's disadvantaged children will therefore help to ensure a more flexible economy tomorrow' (Budget Report, 2003, para. 5.4). But children may just want to make friends!

Conclusion

It is important to note that whilst notions of investment were apparent from Beveridge's Report onwards, children were generally neglected in social policy developments. This has changed and with it important opportunities and difficulties have been opened up. Many of the opportunities and difficulties are the subject of subsequent chapters. Some general points in relation to 'family policy' have emerged in this chapter.

Parents are mobilised in terms of responsibilities towards children. A key responsibility is economic but there are important and ongoing developments to extend parental responsibility for children's behaviour and welfare. There has been an attempt to alter the balance between state and parental responsibilities to a limited extent, with a range of supports in relation to child care and family-friendly policies, but developments remain timid and much of what has occurred seems more concerned with ensuring the production of flexible self-reliant citizens than engaging with how parents and children construct their support needs.

It is no longer accurate to characterise the UK as a place with no or implicit family policies (Land, 1999). There are clearly articulated policies and initiatives which are not about supporting a particular family form but contain a strong reordering impetus. This reordering is concerned not only with behaviour within and between family members but also with identity construction.

CHAPTER 4

Child Abuse and Child Welfare

Child abuse is a term which has occasioned considerable debate at a range of levels, particularly since the 1970s. Definitional questions have been very important as they have keyed into fundamental questions about causation, which link to wider debates about child welfare, the role of the state and the rights and responsibilities of parents and children. In this chapter, we provide a brief overview of such debates since the establishment of the post-war welfare state and explore how child abuse has been conceptualised, particularly in terms of its interrelationship with children's welfare.

The main focus of the chapter is on the developments under New Labour. The abolition of children's poverty through a variety of measures is central to the New Labour agenda, as is *early intervention* to prevent children achieving poorly at school and engaging in anti-social or criminal behaviour. This agenda can contribute to opening up understandings of child abuse in ways which were hinted at in the latter part of Conservative rule and which have been argued for by critics over a number of years. However, there are also dangers in this approach. One is that there seems little commitment to understanding and tackling the complexity of harms that children can suffer in a variety of settings. This is related to and contributes to the rather narrow constructions of parents on which policies are based. Given the centrality of parents to the New Labour agenda in relation to children, these are not incidental criticisms. A further problem concerns a limited engagement with the complexity of children's lives, which means that contemporary policy attaches little priority to addressing the concerns of those children who become caught up in contemporary child protection systems. In short, the dominance of notions of investment militates against developing a project of cultural change in relation to how children are viewed more generally. It is important to note, however, that the Green Paper *Every Child Matters* published in September 2002 would, at first glance, seem to mark something of a shift in relation to the dominance of notions of investment. Its elaboration of a vision for children, seemingly rooted in consultation with them, encompasses a range of outcomes and is both ambitious and wide ranging. However, as will be discussed further in this chapter, the strategies being developed continue to highlight the importance of the priorities attached to the building of a social investment state.

Post-war developments: the 'welfare state'

Clarke *et al.* (2000) explore the centrality of particular assumptions about family, work and nation to the construction and development of the post-war welfare state (see also Williams, 1989; Newman, 2001). The expansion of state provision at this time was framed by the presumption 'that most welfare needs would be satisfied by the family and the market' (Clarke *et al.*, 2000, p. 37). This approach resulted in anomalies such as the splitting of the care and education of children, as we indicated in Chapter 3 (Daniel and Ivatts, 1998; Land, 2002).

Hendrick (1994) argues that the welfare of children was not much more than an afterthought in the grand schemes which brought in the welfare state. There was some concern for the plight of those who could not return home following evacuation, which fed into discussions about other children who were unable to live at home, the nature of post-war child care services and who should be responsible for them. The main role of the Children's Officers employed under the 1948 Children Act appeared to be to prevent children from being removed from their families. Over time, Children's Officers could offer material help as well as casework in support of such aims. Until the 1970s, there was little regard for arguments that children might be endangered by the desire to keep families together (Hendrick, 1994).

Parton (1985) traces the emergence of renewed concerns about the 'abuse' of children within families in the 1960s and particularly in the 1970s. He locates this concern within a series of panics about changes in the family and a so-called decline in law and order. Certainly, the 'discovery' of the 'battered baby syndrome' by medical professionals such as Kempe *et al.* (1962) in the early 1960s was important in directing attention to intra-familial physical abuse and constructing it as a medical/therapeutic problem. Numerous critiques of that analysis and of the attendant treatments have been developed (Parton, 1985; Dale *et al.*, 1986; Featherstone, 1997).

In the early 1970s, the death of Maria Colwell at the hands of her stepfather and the subsequent public inquiry was to occasion enormous publicity and to prove decisive in a range of ways. It began a process of regulating the work carried out by child welfare professionals, which impacted particularly on practices in the newly-established local authorities. The 1970s saw the introduction of a range of new policies, practices and procedures (Parton, 2002). Police, social services, paediatricians, health visitors and general practitioners became increasingly subject to guidance, both from local committees and from central government.

Other high-profile inquiries followed in the 1980s. These were all inquiries into child deaths at the hands of parents; or, more accurately, generally men with differing biological relationships to the children. Two of these cases, those of Jasmine Beckford and Tyra Henry, were of black children. Although these were amongst the most high-profile inquiries into child deaths, they were by no means the only ones (Fox Harding, 1991; see also Reder *et al.*, 1993).

Until the late 1980s, all key inquiries involved intra-familial child deaths where there had been some level of professional, crucially social work, involvement. The attendant publicity and specific recommendations led to further guidance and regulations from government alongside a revision of social work education. Until 1989, it is possible to argue that the inquiries promoted the following construction of 'child abuse': it was physical in nature, carried out by parents or carers and was preventable if professionals did the right things. Thus, the emergence of a discourse on 'child protection' which led to an emphasis on professional in action, as distinct from thinking about why children might be harmed by adults in the first instance.

However, the public inquiry into the handling of sexual abuse cases in Cleveland in the northeast of England at the end of the 1980s was to disrupt this analysis to some extent (Corby, 2002). This inquiry was concerned with what key professionals had done rather than not done – which was to remove over 100 children in a fairly short period of time from their parents, because of concerns about sexual abuse (Campbell, 1988). Cleveland destabilised key components of the earlier analysis and introduced uncertainty: uncertainty as a consequence of recognising the complexity of differing forms of child maltreatment and uncertainty in terms of whether there was one way of dealing with these complexities. It also brought the notion of children's 'personhood' to the fore, primarily as a result of Justice Butler Schloss's statement at the Inquiry that 'the child should be seen as a person not as an object of concern' (Daniel and Ivatts, 1998).

However, the inquiry did not contribute to any wide-ranging engagement with the subject of sexual abuse itself. Indeed, the question of why it happens did not form part of its remit, which continued a focus on the protection of children as the central task for professionals, rather than an issue requiring broader action, including political and cultural change (Campbell, 1988). The events in Cleveland were to prove significant also in that they were a key impetus behind the then government's decision to commission a wide-ranging research programme (DoH, 1995). The lessons from this programme continue to be influential and will be explored in the section on 'The Children Act' that follows.

Alternative voices

Fox Harding (1991) argues that the 'state paternalism and child protection' perspective, which legitimates extensive state intervention to protect and care for children, emerged in the 1970s in response to the Maria Colwell inquiry. There was a greater emphasis, compared with preceding decades, on protecting children from their families and on the use of substitute care: 'There was also a greater readiness to focus on the child as a separate individual and to act coercively, if need be, on her/his behalf' (p. 91). These tendencies gave rise to a range of criticisms, some of which mapped onto the writings of those within a category identified by Fox Harding as 'the modern defence of the birth family and parents' rights'. For example, Holman (1988) argued that birth or biological family ties should be maintained wherever possible; where families have to be separated, links should be maintained. The role of the state should be neither paternalist nor laissez faire, but supportive of families by providing the various services that families may need in order to remain together. The possibility that children might be harmed within families was not a primary concern of such critics, particularly given the overwhelming evidence that it was poor children who were being taken away from poor parents, a significant proportion of whom were lone mothers from minority ethnic backgrounds (Bebbington and Miles, 1989).

Some of these criticisms mapped onto debates about how child abuse was being defined, why it happened and what should be done about it (Parton, 1985). For example, the role of social policies which contribute to children's poverty was argued to be abusive to children as well as central to the causation of physical abuse. This view was contested by those who argued that the latter argument was unfair to poor people (Fox Harding, 1991). However, the growth of awareness of sexual abuse forced critics such as Parton to rethink their views (Parton, 1990). He recognised that it did not fit clearly into an analysis which focused on poverty as central to the causation of abuse and obliged wider thinking which recognised both gendered and generational power imbalances. His arguments reflected a debt to emerging feminist understandings. These contested the failure of investigations such as the Cleveland Inquiry to explore why it was largely men who engaged in sexually abusive activity and also contested gender-blind professional practices. They argued that it is important to interrogate wider processes in relation to patterns of male socialisation alongside gendered power relations (Featherstone, 2002). Arguments also emerged from those interested in advancing children's rights. These pointed to the lack of power of children as a group, in relation to bodily integrity and voice, as central to understanding why adults transgressed their bodily boundaries and children were unable to assert their rights and claims for recognition (see Fox Harding, 1991).

By the end of the 1980s, physical and sexual abuse were being dealt with by various agencies and there was a large amount of guidance available on how they should work together. There were competing debates about how these forms of abuse should be understood and their interrelationship (see, for example, Hearn, 1990). However, it is possible to argue that the dominant discourses at policy and practice levels were concerned with what should be done by professionals, in relation to managing abuses, and with the appropriate balance which should be struck between state intervention and family privacy. The Children Act (1989) was introduced in this context.

The Children Act

The Children Act emerged from a period of considerable debate and activity and was widely welcomed. It was the product of years of consultation with a range of groups, although not with children (Hendrick, 1994, 2003; Daniel and Ivatts, 1998). The Act brought together public and private law and sought to establish a new basis for intervention in family life in cases of child abuse – by placing the courts at the centre of the process . It also sought to establish a mandate for supportive work for children 'in need'.

A number of key principles underpinned the Act. One of these was that the child's welfare should be the paramount consideration. This principle was to govern both the making of orders in private cases such as divorce and the decisions on whether to place a child in local authority care or supervision. This obliged professionals to justify their decision-making. There was also an obligation that the ascertainable wishes and feelings of the child should be considered in making decisions, which helped to make children more central to proceedings. Guardians ad litem, court-appointed social workers specifically representing the child's interests, played an important role: 'The fact that children were to have their own advocate in court proceedings served to strengthen and underline the idea of children as individuals in their own right with interests which might be quite separate from those of their parents' (Daniel and Ivatts, 1998, p. 206).

The Act also introduced the concept of parental responsibility into the process. As Fox Harding (1996) noted, since 1979 the Conservatives had developed an interest in the issue of family responsibility, in the scope of state responsibility and, in particular, in the amount of state expenditure involved in the latter:

> A rhetoric of family behaviour has been developed in which certain themes, such as individual responsibility and the undesirability of dependence on the state, have become central to the aim of restoring or revitalizing family responsibility. A major preoccupation has been the area of parental responsibility (p. 130).

As was noted in Chapter 3, parental responsibility became a theme uniting a range of legislation in the late 1980s and 1990s. Harding argued that whilst the different types of parental responsibility were not always consistent, the concept was used 'as a powerful instrument of social policy in shaping the family' (Edwards and Halpern, 1992, quoted in Fox Harding, 1996). It meshed with a wider strategy which promoted more private dependency within families, fewer state-dependent families and broader family responsibility.

Parton has argued that the notion of parental responsibility in the Children Act reflected both wider historical tendencies and the prevailing Conservative political agenda:

> While the family was constructed as an essentially private institution and the primary institution for rearing children, parents were seen as having responsibilities towards their children, rather than holding in effect, parental property rights as in the past. The role of parents was cast in far more active terms, and terms consistent with the government emphasis on individuals and families taking responsibility for both their own behaviour and the quality of life of their dependents. While the state was seen as having an important role to play, this was to ensure that parents fulfilled such responsibilities. The role of the state was confirmed as residual and supportive rather than primary. However, it should work in partnership with parents on behalf of children in need. (Parton, 1991, p. 155)

A key space for inquiring and exploring what was happening with the implementation of the Act was provided by the publication of Messages from Research: Lessons for Child Protection (DoH, 1995).

Messages from research – reconstructing child abuse?

Following the Cleveland Inquiry, the then Conservative government commissioned a range of research studies into how the child protection system operated and was perceived alongside more wide-ranging studies into the use of discipline in 'normal' family life and into sexual abuse. The results were published with considerable fanfare in 1995, in an overview document summarising the research studies and their key messages (DoH, 1995).

John Bowis, the then Minister of State, argued in the overview document that the key message emanating from the studies was that the spirit of the Children Act was not being adhered to. The spirit of the Act, he argued, was that there should be a balance between child protection and family support services. However, in practice what appeared to be happening was that child protection investigations were being prioritised, leading to a distortion of the system's workload and with little priority being devoted to preventive or supportive work. Moreover, such investigations were being conducted in a way which alienated parents and children. Bowis argued for a shift in emphasis from child protection to family support and encouraged local authorities to review and reorient their service provision accordingly.

An approach was promoted which moved away from the investigation of specific incidents of abuse in favour of exploring such incidents in context and was generally more supportive and responsive to families' overall needs. This should have implications for practice at every stage, from what became known as the 'enquiry' phase right through to ongoing support. This approach contributed to a reconstruction of child abuse so that it ceased to be solely focused on specific incidents. Such incidents should be located in the context of the overall environment in which the child lived; specific contexts which were low in warmth and high in criticism were seen as particularly deleterious. This analysis fed into a growing recognition of the interrelationships between different forms of harm. As part of this process, emotional abuse and neglect become more firmly recognised (see Cawson *et al.*, 2000 for a very thorough discussion).

However, the analysis did not significantly broaden out what might be considered abusive. The issues thrown up by decades of inattention by government to issues of poverty and inequality were inadequately addressed. Child poverty had increased considerably under the Conservatives and, as we saw in the last chapter, there had been significant changes in family structure. Such changes are strongly correlated with poverty, so practitioners were encountering complex family structures and widespread levels of poverty alongside a lack of any supportive infrastructure in terms of service provision. Encouraging an orientation to 'family' support begged crucial questions in a world where notions of family had become more complex and resources in relation to the professional provision of support were thin on the ground.

There were also problems with the actual research done and the way in which it was disseminated. It did nothing to redress the lack of a research base which looked systematically at both prevalence and incidence issues in relation to child abuse or which ascertained from children and young people themselves what their experiences and definitions were (see discussion below). A key problem which was addressed by only some of the research and which was certainly not highlighted in the dissemination process is that focusing on what professionals do or do not do in relation to referrals gives us a very partial picture. There is ample evidence, for example, that the majority of those who are sexually abused never approach professionals at all. Indeed, Wattam's (2002) research highlights the very low levels of self-referral by children to the formal child protection system.

Furthermore, the dissemination process and the central thrust of the overview document promoted a fairly singular and simplified story about practice within the system and how it should be reoriented. Child protection was constructed as a largely policing, reactive activity and was counterposed to a more desirable approach called family support, thus contributing to a form of split thinking which has proved more and more problematic over time (see, for example, DoH, 2001b). In the overview document, there was an absence of any adequate contextual analysis of why practice might have developed in the way it had and the significant omission of any analysis of the impact of the inquiries into child deaths (Parton, 1996). Also important was the failure to explore the impact of successive cuts in government spending on mainstream services such as social work and the lack of bridging finance for local authorities seeking to implement the Children Act, of the kind that had been provided for Community Care legislation (see Gardner, 2002).

As indicated, the causes of differing forms of child abuse did not form part of the remit; the primary focus was on what was being done or not done by professionals. The analysis screened out key questions in relation to wider social policies and inequalities. However, there was ample evidence from the individual research reports themselves of the impact of poverty and gender issues (Parton, 1996). For example, 'conflict' and 'violence' between adult men and women were important features of many of the cases studied. This did not lead to widespread discussion about whether the origins of such violence might lie beyond the individual couple in an interrogation of relationships between men and women.

Prior to the election of New Labour, the following was apparent. Governmental injunctions to develop 'family support' coexisted with very high levels of inequality and poverty promoted by the very same government's policies. Family structures had changed considerably and notions of parental responsibilities had been extended in a context where little support for discharging such responsibilities had been developed and there was little commitment to dealing with the gendered implications of exercising such responsibilities.

Also, there was a questioning of the value of constructing child abuse narrowly in terms of incidents of abuse but no real appreciation on the part of government that a more thorough engagement with the complexities behind definition and causation was required. Family support was pulled out of the hat as an almost magical means of reconciling considerable tensions, legitimating assumptions that all that was needed was a change of attitude by social workers.

What has happened under New Labour?

Whilst no clear statements have been made by New Labour about how they understand child abuse and what should be done about it, there are signals. The predominant concerns in relation to children's welfare are ending their poverty and early intervention in relation to facilitating their life chances. These are supported by a research base and there is a commitment by the government to monitor what is happening through its Opportunity for All Reports (see Chapter 1).

However, government has done nothing to rectify the lack of government statistics which show the number of children who experience a range of harms in a range of settings. The one indicator which is used in the Opportunity for All Reports is that of reducing re-registration rates on the child protection register – an indicator which has been used to monitor both local authority and Sure Start activities. The Child Protection Register (originally called the Child Abuse Register) was set up in the 1970s in the plethora of procedures which emerged following the death of Maria Colwell. It is an administrative device deployed by professionals to indicate that there are concerns about, or there has been actual, abuse and should be tied to a plan of work to protect the child/children. For a host of reasons, monitoring registrations or re-registrations is very unsatisfactory (see Jeffery, 2003). Registration rates are probably likely to tell us more about the ways in which agencies work than about what is actually happening to children. A finding that re-registration rates are falling may therefore reflect agencies' neglect of children rather than more positive processes.

Hooper (2002) has attempted to develop some data in relation to rates of fatal child abuse, physical punishment and abuse, physical neglect, sexual abuse and emotional maltreatment, including exposure to domestic violence between parents. She notes the difficulties in relying on any form of official statistics. As only a small number of incidents are reported to any agency, reliance on agency statistics such as those provided by the police or social services is very problematic. Moreover, the attrition rate is high and variable between areas and forms of abuse. Some offences, such as rape, are not broken down by age.

As Hooper argues, to get any sense of the extent and patterns of child maltreatment it is necessary to turn to non-governmental research (although there is still a paucity of such research in the UK). The most comprehensive, methodologically sophisticated study was that undertaken by the National Society for the Prevention of Cruelty to Children (NSPCC) and published in 2000. This looked at the experiences of just under 3000 young people aged between 18 and 24 (Cawson *et al.*, 2000). Even here, the findings are likely to be an underestimate as the sample excluded those who were homeless or in institutional settings. Fifty-six per cent of the sample were still living with their parents and there were likely to be problems with the recall of past events. Nonetheless, the study is well worth exploring in detail as it offers important discussions about how varying forms of abuse were defined as well as contrasting researcher definitions with self-definitions by respondents. Only a brief picture can be offered here, in conjunction with Hooper's (2002) review of what is currently known in relation to various forms of maltreatment.

In terms of fatal child abuse, there have been considerable debates about both the evidence and the trends. In relation to the latter, Pritchard's (1992) findings that there had been a decline from the 1970s to the 1980s have been strongly contested by children's charities such as the NSPCC. As Hooper notes, the decline now seems largely attributable to changes in the system for classification. There is a commonly cited estimate that one to two children die from maltreatment each week and rates appear to have stayed stable during the 1980s and 1990s. However, Hooper (2002) outlines the limitations of the statistics and there is some reason to believe that they underestimate the numbers of such deaths.

In terms of other forms of maltreatment, physical abuse is particularly difficult to define, since hitting a child can still be defended in court by a parent as 'reasonable chastisement'. According to Cawson *et al.* (2000), 25 per cent in their sample had experienced some form of physical abuse which ranged in terms of severity. Sixteen per cent of the sample had experienced some form of sexually abusive activity. The study contains a very important discussion on the difficulties of defining emotional maltreatment and is a considered contribution to thinking in this area. Bullying emerged as by far the most common area of difficulty experienced by young people, with 43 per cent having experienced some form of bullying by another young person. Twenty-six per cent had experienced violence between their adult carers at some point and for 5 per cent this was constant or frequent. The rates of such violence are possibly declining but they still remain higher than in the 1980s (see Hooper, 2002 for a discussion; also Mirrlees-Black, 1999).

New Labour has not placed any priority on developing a better information base in relation to the range of harms that children can suffer. It has also seemed content in large part to continue with the Children Act 1989, although there have been important legislative developments in relation to adoption and leaving care (see Chapter 5) and a legislative amendment which reflects the harms to children caused by violence between adult carers is planned. The Protection of Children Act 1999 introduced a number of changes to the system for vetting and identifying unsuitable persons working with children and a Sexual Offences Bill was introduced in order to consolidate and update legislation in relation to sexual offending against adults and children.

In terms of guidance documents from government, two have been particularly influential. These are the Framework for the Assessment of Children in Need and their Families (DoH, 2000a) and Working Together to Safeguard the Welfare of Children in Need and their Families (DoH, Home Office, DfEE, 1999).

An important development at the policy implementation level has been the establishment of a Children's Taskforce focused on improving health and social care services. An early task assigned to it was the completion of a National Service Framework for Children (similar frameworks have been introduced for mental health, coronary heart disease, older people's services and diabetes) to set new standards across the National Health Service and social services for children.

Discussion

To some extent, New Labour has exhibited continuities with the previous Conservative administration in relation to tackling child abuse. In particular, much of their analysis has been couched in language borrowed directly from the analysis outlined in Messages from Research (DoH, 1995). For example, their report submitted to the UN Committee on the Rights of the Child in 1999 (there is a requirement that a report is submitted every 5 years) argued that physical and sexual abuse within the home is often triggered by pressure on families and 'real benefits could arise if there was a focus on the wider needs of children and families, rather than a narrow concentration on the alleged incident of abuse' (quoted in Roberts, 2001, p. 59).

However, in contrast to previous Conservative governments, New Labour has taken seriously the issue of the 'context' in which family life is lived and the welfare of children more generally. Preventive strategies are strongly underlined in the New Labour project. Important examples of this approach include Sure Start and the Children's Fund. While these do not have an *overt* agenda in relation to preventing child abuse, there can be a presumption that this will be a by-product of their activities. The eradication of poverty, for example, can be framed in this way; though, as we have seen, the role of poverty as a causal factor in relation to the range of harms children can suffer has been disputed by researchers over the years.

The priorities for what needs to be prevented are attached very firmly to the priorities of a social investment state: preventing future unemployment and the involvement of children in criminal and anti-social behaviour. Furthermore, they are accompanied by a redefinition of prevention itself which emphasises earlier identification of those 'at risk'. Indeed, considerable work is being undertaken on the development of identification, referral and tracking systems (IRT) to aid early identification of those truanting, engaging in anti-social activity and so on.

There are omissions in Labour's understandings and strategies which have particular implications for child maltreatment. The failure to legislate against smacking remains a constant source of criticism of New Labour – the critics include those monitoring the UNCRC (see Featherstone *et al.*, 2002), children's organisations and parliamentary groups. These criticisms have received renewed impetus as a result of the death of Victoria Climbié in 2000 from a range of abusive treatments by her great aunt and her great aunt's partner. This particular death has been cited as an illustration of the dangers of not firmly opposing the use of physical force against any child for any reason, including 'reasonable chastisement'. There is a strong argument for such a ban, not just in terms of possibly preventing such deaths but also as part of a wider political and cultural project which gives out clear messages about children and adult/child relationships.

Also, there is a silence on the importance of challenging gendered aspects of sexual violence. The finding that those who sexually abuse are predominantly male appears to be a strong one, although there are limitations in the data currently available (Frosh, 2002). Yet this appears to have led to little in the way of prevention campaigns which tackle gendered attitudes to violence and sexuality. Furthermore, an understanding of gender relations would be helpful in terms of understanding the levels of abuse between young people themselves that were found within the prevalence study discussed above (Cawson *et al.*, 2000). Whilst anti-bullying strategies have been developed by New Labour and are welcome, they need to be more fully informed by understandings which locate sexual violence as an aspect of bullying and which also engage with what appears to be differences in male and female patterns of coping and help seeking amongst young people (Hallett *et al.*, 2003).

There are also more general issues which need exploring in relation to children's help seeking. New Labour has paid little attention to tackling the difficulties which have emerged over the decades in relation to how children use and perceive the formal systems set up to protect them.

The child protection system – protecting who from what?

Under New Labour, some important initiatives have emerged in relation to ensuring that children who are looked after (that is, come into some form of state care; see Chapter 5) are consulted with in relation to the experience of being looked after. Many of these children will have been abused and subject to child protection investigations and assessments. However, many other children who have been subject to such investigations and processes do not come under the looked after system.

In previous sections, we outlined how developments in the 1970s and 1980s had led to a complex system focused on managing what professionals did in response to referrals. Not only have children not been involved in designing this system, there are also clear indications that they remain profoundly unhappy with aspects of it. In particular, the importance attached to the sharing of information between professionals runs counter to what research tells us about the importance that children and young people attach to confidentiality (see MacLeod, 1999).

The issue of confidentiality appears central to why children who are suffering maltreatment do not approach professionals. Child-Line, a confidential and anonymous telephone helpline, has been used in large numbers by children and young people since its inception over 10 years ago. Research on its use offers us access to information about the definitions of abuse used by children and also to their ideas about how they might best be helped. Moreover, ChildLine's continued success in engaging children and young people in large numbers would appear to provide some indication about what they find helpful about a service set up and run by adults. The issue of confidentiality is crucial and is tested out time and time again by the children who call. The form of help offered appears to be appreciated – it is at the young person's pace, and space is offered to talk over issues rather than rush into action. This is in contrast to how professional services are perceived to operate. In particular, in relation to sexual abuse, there continues to be a premium placed by professionals on 'doing something' fast and alerting professional networks (Parton and Wattam, 1999).

Hill (1997b) has reviewed the research which has been carried out into the views of those who do refer or are referred to the child protection system. This reveals considerable criticisms of the overall experience, although the majority said that they had no regrets about speaking out. However, there was a minority who found the official response to abuse allegations so upsetting that they did regret it. Many indicated they were given little information and few choices, and a general picture emerges of children caught up in a perplexing and distressing sequence of events (Featherstone and Parton, 2001).

The Department of Health was, until June 2003, the key government department responsible for child protection work. It devoted very little attention to addressing how child protection processes could become more child-friendly and did not initiate a debate on the difficult issue of confidentiality; of how to ensure that more children and young people could be encouraged to raise their concerns about child maltreatment and how such concerns could then be worked with in ways which ensured that they felt some control over what happened. This is difficult terrain and some of the dilemmas may not be resolvable. There are many arguments in favour of having an effective system of information sharing, not least that it facilitates a holistic understanding of a child's difficulties. However, it is also apparent that children and young people do not use formal systems because of concerns about confidentiality.

A key document produced by New Labour has been the Framework for the Assessment of Children in Need and their Families (DoH, 2000a). This appears to reinforce the importance of locating children and their families contextually rather than looking at incidents of abuse in isolation. It contains many references to the centrality of the child and the importance of consulting with him or her. However, it assumes that needs, including the need for protection, can be accessed by professionals both asking and observing and/or can be articulated by children. In contrast, research into child sexual abuse seems to indicate that the process of telling is extremely complex and profoundly influenced relational and contextual factors (Wattam, 1999). Moreover, in the absence of a narrative by children, professionals cannot rely on looking for 'signs' of sexual abuse in any straightforward way. Such signs are highly contested, as events in Cleveland demonstrated. The Framework bypasses key questions about who can be told what and in what contexts (see Wattam, 1999). It not only ignores the research evidence which indicates that children do not trust professionals, but also assumes that changing language and focusing on need is enough to encourage children to talk openly to professionals about what is troubling them.

It could be argued that the general message from Messages from Research – promoting a move-away from a child protection approach which is investigatory and driven by forensic requirements in relation to proof – could meet many of the concerns identified by children when they enter the system. However, one can doubt whether the solution promoted by Messages from Research – a move to family support – will ensure that children's wishes are taken into account.

This is a particularly apt question to consider in the context of New Labour's approach to parents. Where parents are themselves the direct cause of the harms that children suffer, this is explained in government guidance in terms of them being 'under stress' and the assumption appears to be that the overall agenda in relation to challenging poverty and social exclusion will remove such stress (see, for example, Framework for the Assessment of Children in Need and their Families and Working Together to Safeguard the Welfare of Children). There is no discussion about whether such abuses could be linked with gendered and generational dynamics which render children unable to assert their rights to bodily integrity and voice.

As was noted in Chapter 3, the roles and responsibilities of parents are central to delivering much of the New Labour agenda in relation to children. As Freely (2000) notes, this is often a top-down agenda which is not located in ongoing dialogue with parents. For example, parents' own definitions of what is considered responsible parental behaviour are not always recognised as such by the government (see Duncan and Edwards, 1999 for a general discussion of this in relation to lone mothers and paid work). An example here is that the focus on moving adults on benefits, including lone mothers, into employment as a key way of tackling poverty and the impact in situations where abuse and violence is a feature of family life has not been considered. For example, compatible welfare developments in the US appear to have contributed to difficulties for women who are required by one set of policies to enter paid work and another to be available to protect their children (Brandwein, 1999). Whilst policies for moving young mothers into work in the UK, unlike those in the US, are not compulsory, the current emphasis on the desirability of entering paid work is feared by many mothers of children who have been sexually abused. Their definition of responsibility is that they need time to spend with their children and to look after them in order to engage with the healing and protection issues which will be thrown up. This neglect is not accidental, since engaging with such issues is quite simply not a priority for New Labour.

Tensions in practice

A range of initiatives have been set up outside local authority structures (see Jordan and Jordan, 2000; Garrett, 2002, for a general discussion). Some of what has happened under New Labour could be seen as a response to the perceived failure by local authorities to refocus in the way that was argued for under Messages from Research. Moreover, it is possible to see more recent developments as New Labour quietly giving up the ghost on social services departments and transferring the mandate for supportive and preventive work to various 'new' initiatives. A key reason for the emergence of these 'new' initiatives, however, may be that they focus on different and, by definition, more desirable priorities from those of local authority social work. Social work was tied in, often uneasily, with the priorities of the old welfare state. In contrast, the new initiatives are part of a broader project – that of constructing self-reliant, employable individuals who are flexible enough to operate effectively in the global order. The use of 'old' terms, such as family support, can therefore prove misleading. However, this is by no means made clear cut or explicit in practice, leaving local authority social services departments with confused messages.

Moreover, the split which emerged post-Messages from Research between child protection and family support can institutionalise a binary approach to children and families which does not correspond with how they live their lives and encounter difficulties. Children's needs cannot be categorised simply in terms of either protection or support and there are real dangers in encouraging such binary thinking. To give an example, domestic violence is recognised as a widespread phenomenon and one which can have adverse effects upon children's welfare as well as their safety. Sure Start projects with a family support remit, but with no targets in relation to domestic violence, are discovering the need to work with domestic violence if they are to be responsive to their local communities and therefore are working with protection and support issues. Neat categorisations do not work in practice in a world where violence and abuse cannot be simply ascribed to a small number of highly stressed families.

The emergence of 'new' initiatives on the ground involves considerable numbers of workers in a period where there are problems with retention and recruitment in mainstream services, such as local authority social and health visiting. There is evidence that many of the new initiatives are contributing to this crisis in that they are recruiting workers from the mainstream (Garrett, 2002). At the same time, we continue to have a system which is led by social services departments but premised upon inter-agency working and which has developed procedures and guidance in relation to managing and working with child protection concerns which require considerable resourcing.

The inquiry into the death of Victoria Climbié, which was published in 2003, opened up possibilities for discussing such issues. The inquiry itself had an interesting format, with Part 1 exploring what happened to Victoria via the questioning of key witnesses (including those convicted of her death). Part 2 was organised in the form of seminars focused on particular topics.

A range of recommendations emerged which, in the main, concentrated on two areas; accountability for work and clarifying procedures for dealing with referrals (see Laming, 2003). Whilst issues such as recruitment were mentioned, as well as the damaging consequences of splits between child protection and family support, there was little discussion about the overall policy context and how well it supported the discussions and initiatives necessary to tackle the range of harms that children suffer. Although the death of Victoria has provided added impetus for campaigning against the use of smacking (Hall, 2003), the report itself did not engage with such debates.

The government's reorganisation of children's services announced in June 2003 offers an opportunity to pull together a range of services on education and care – although young offenders are not included. A Minister for Children and Young People has been appointed with specific responsibilities for the following: Sure Start, Early Years, Connexions, Special Educational Needs and the Youth Service, the Children and Young People's Unit, the Children's Social Services and the Teenage Pregnancy Unit, Family and Parenting Law and Support and the Family Policy Unit. This poses both opportunities as well as dangers, as outlined in Chapter 3 – more integrated approaches to the care and education of children may emerge but a focus on education and skills may contribute to narrow, instrumentalist initiatives.

The Green Paper *Every Child Matters*, published in 2003 (DfES, 2003b), emerged initially from a concern to try and develop a coherent approach to the proliferation of initiatives for children at risk of social exclusion. However, the publication of the report by Lord Laming into the death of Victoria Climbie early in 2003 seemed to force the government, initially at least, to indicate that it would incorporate its response into the Green Paper. In the event, its response was actually published alongside the Green Paper as a separate document, *Keeping Children Safe*. This would indicate that, alongside its separate response to youth offending (see Chapter 6), it continues to have difficulty with developing an integrated response to children as a whole. Moreover, within the Green Paper there is a failure to look at the variety of harms children can suffer and there seems to be an overemphasis on tacking their educational difficulties at the expense of other issues which barely get mentioned, such as sexual abuse. Furthermore, there appears little recognition of the need to develop initiatives which are underpinned by robust research evidence into children's experiences, including their experiences of harm and what they wish from adults.

Conclusion

This chapter has traced how 'child abuse' has been variously constructed over the decades, since the establishment of the post-war welfare state. It argues that developments under New Labour open up welcome opportunities for tackling children's poverty, thus potentially contributing in important ways to the enhancement of children's overall welfare. Alongside the array of initiatives outlined in Chapter 3 which offer parents supports to bring up their children, these can be viewed positively. However, there is too little attention being paid to the variety of harms children suffer and to the reform of the systems which have been set up to 'protect' them from such arms. A number of key omissions are highly significant. The failure to legislate against smacking indicates both an unwillingness to challenge generational power imbalances and to signpost the need for more democratic practices between adults and children. This reflects a reluctance to move away from a populist project which seeks to woo rather than lead and rests on what may be profoundly mistaken assumptions about parents' own views. The assumption is that parents will not tolerate such state interference in their relationships with their children – this needs further testing. Furthermore, allied with this appears to be a lack of interest in thinking about how the systems which have developed over the years can be made more child friendly, thus leaving us with the undesirable situation of having child protection systems in which children do not appear to invest.

There has been an extension of state involvement in children's and families' lives, primarily within a project aimed at getting poor parents to fulfil their responsibilities towards their children and which is overly-focused on instrumental approaches which produce self-reliant citizens. A broader project, which seeks to explore how children are harmed in a variety of settings and what their views are of what should be done about it, does not appear to be part of the New Labour agenda.

CHAPTER 5

Looked After Children

Introduction

This chapter is concerned with recent policy and practice developments with respect to those children whose lives are most intimately bound to the actions of the state – those who live directly under its care. The chapter focuses primarily on policy towards looked after children in England. Scotland has different and distinctive practices and legislation in this field and Wales itself is now increasingly deserving of separate attention as the Welsh Assembly forges different approaches in social care. For example, Wales decided to appoint a Children's Commissioner for all children in 2000, whereas England did not do so until 2003. Wales also has a separate strategy for social services for children, 'Children First'.

If we consider this group of children in relation to the central tendencies in New Labour policy that were identified in Chapter 1, a number of issues become immediately apparent. With respect to the emphasis on parents as the key means for ensuring child welfare, there are obvious difficulties of application in a context in which children are no longer (in most cases) living with their parents but instead live within a variety of alternative settings – primarily foster care and residential care. Fox Harding (1997, pp. 182–185) notes that in some respects the 1989 Children Act strengthened the rights of parents in the social care context and encouraged social services to work in partnership with families. However, for many children entering the care system, parental indifference or abuse is likely to be more relevant than parental involvement. This lowered involvement of parents gave scope for a stronger state-paternalist agenda for New Labour in the late 1990s than would have been possible in fields with strong parental and family lobby groups, a paternalism that was reminiscent of Labour's more interventionist past.

Nevertheless, a strong focus on parenting and on the family is evident in this context through an increased emphasis on the importance of foster care and through a renewed focus on adoption as a long-term solution to the problems of some looked after children. This leaves us with two contrasting, and to some extent conflicting, models of parenting. The first is the use of families, family substitutes or family models where appropriate and the second is the use of the state to ensure adequate 'corporate parenting'. The concept of 'corporate parenting' has been applied to this field through both the QP initiative (seeking to pressure local authorities to perform the caring duties of a 'good parent') and the Children (Leaving Care) Act 2000 (seeking to compel local authorities to apply such 'good parenting' for longer than hitherto).

The second feature of our analysis of New Labour's approach, its focus on targeting specific groups of children for policy attention, is perhaps nowhere better illustrated than with respect to looked after children. As with Sure Start, there is – as we shall see – a very strong 'social investment' rationale for doing so. It has also led to a strong form of managerial control through the QP initiative. While we can see the implications of this approach in a number of other chapters, the clear realisation by the late 1990s of the stark social consequences of neglecting the needs of looked after children led to a particularly clear rationale for significant action in this field. There are, of course – as we saw in Chapter 2 – problems associated with an approach that views children primarily as arenas for investment in the future. However, it can still be argued that the social investment model has produced much more policy attention to both the present and future needs of this group of children than had previously been the case.

Finally, with respect to New Labour's piecemeal approach to the application of a children's rights perspective, it is in relation to looked after children that it has been most distinctively positive. A combination of acknowledged poor performance, widespread abuse scandals and the reduced relevance of the parent–child axis in this arena has led the New Labour government to a much easier acceptance of the right of children to participate in decision-making processes affecting their lives. By making such participation a key objective of the QP initiative, the UK government has sought to raise the profile of children's rights in this area within local government social services departments.

Accordingly, this chapter charts a period of vigorous activity on the part of government in recent years. We begin by outlining the key developments in fields such as the education of looked after children, leaving care, the overall framework of QP, the increased governmental interest in adoption and the development of a new inspection and regulation regime. The impact of these initiatives is then assessed. This assessment includes consideration of the implications of these developments for subjects such as children's rights and involvement, the developing role of the family and the role of the state.

Tackling social exclusion: focusing on looked after children

Looked after children have been a subject of growing concern for UK governments since the early 1990s and were the focus of particularly intense policy interest by the post-1997 New Labour government, leading to a number of significant initiatives. These include new guidance on the education of looked after children (Department of Health and Department for Education and Employment, 2000), the QP initiative, the Children (Leaving Care) Act 2000 and, in part, the Care Standards Act 2000 and the Adoption and Children Act 2002. However, the significance of New Labour's policy approach to looked after children to its own definition of its overall project was missed by many commentators: New Labour's policies for children in public care received more coverage in its own 2001 General Election Manifesto (Labour Party, 2001, pp. 27–28) than they did in a number of the lengthier academic commentaries on the party's first term (Coates and Lawler, 2000; Seldon, 2001; Powell, 2002), which failed to even refer to the above initiatives. Only Toynbee and Walker's analysis of the 1997–2001 government adequately reflected the symbolic and practical importance of this subject to New Labour's wider strategy for child welfare (Toynbee and Walker, 2001, pp. 34–36).

Underpinning New Labour's concern was the extent to which this client group illustrates both the perceived and the real failings of the post-war model of welfare state provision. The top-down, bureaucratic, secretive and unresponsive welfare state criticised by both right and left from the 1970s onwards can be argued to have reached its nadir with the treatment of looked after children, as revealed by the repeated revelations of widespread and hidden abuse within the state child care system that emerged during the 1990s (Levy and Kahan, 1991; Kirkwood, 1993; Utting, 1997; Waterhouse, 2000). Alongside the various abuse scandals, cumulative evidence of failure on a less dramatic but equally important front – outcomes for looked after children in areas such as employment, education and housing (Biehal *et al.*, 1995; Broad, 1998; Smith, 1998) – linked this area more directly to New Labour's wider concern with both social exclusion and social investment. One illustration of this linkage is that looked after children were identified as an especially vulnerable group in each of the first three reports from the government's Social Exclusion Unit. The first of these reports, on truancy and school exclusion, pointed out that children in care are 'ten times more likely' than average to be excluded from school (Social Exclusion Unit, 1998a, p. 9). The second report, on rough sleeping, noted that 'between a quarter and a third of rough sleepers have been looked after by local authorities as children' (Social Exclusion Unit, 1998b, p. 5) and cited the early age of discharge and lack of support for care leavers as crucial factors. The third report, on teenage pregnancy, cited research suggesting that 'a quarter of care leavers had a child by the age of sixteen, and nearly half were mothers within 18 to 24 months after leaving care' (Social Exclusion Unit, 1999, p. 17).

Even before these reports, a ubiquitous set of statistics had began to be widely quoted in official sources – despite many of them being rather vague estimates (the lack of hard data about this group being, indeed, indicative of their relative neglect). Amongst the best known of these statistics were that between 50 and 75 per cent of care leavers had no academic qualifications (compared to 6 per cent in the general population), that 50–80 per cent of care leavers were unemployed (at a time when it was below 15 per cent in the general population of the same age), that 23 per cent of adult prisoners and 38 per cent of young prisoners have been in care, that 30 per cent of the young single homeless had a care background and that almost all care leavers exit into 'independence' by the age of 18 (the average age of leaving home in the general population in the late 1990s was 22) (Social Services Inspectorate, 1997; Utting, 1997). That the numbers of children in care represent only 0.5 per cent of the relevant age group (Sinclair and Gibbs, 2002, p. 123) serves to indicate the depths of the problems that these statistics represent. In short, looked after children and care leavers represent a 'sticking point' on the road to an economically and socially successful society of the kind that is consistent with New Labour's 'Third Way'. As a group, their multiple disadvantages rendered them particularly worthy of targeted interventions. They overlapped with the government's agendas on homelessness, youth unemployment, youth justice, low educational attainment and teenage pregnancy. If Sure Start offered an opportunity for productive investment because it focused on the influential early years of a child's life, policies for looked after children offered a similarly productive opportunity because of the breadth of the contact with social exclusion. The enhanced governmental interest in this group can also be explained on the basis that, because they are already in the care of the State, this is a group of socially excluded young people that is particularly amenable to state investment. These two factors combined – the range of their problems and their openness to state activism – rendered them a particularly productive opportunity for social investment.

Past policy towards looked after children

Many histories of UK policy towards looked after children begin with the post-1945 Labour government; with good reason, even though there is much that can usefully be learnt from earlier periods. The work of the Curtis Committee and the establishment of local authority children's departments by the 1948 Children Act marked a decisive break with the institutions (though not always the ethos) of Work House and Poor Law. This was exemplified by the decades-long switch towards smaller, more homely institutions, epitomised by the 'family group home' of the 1970s and the increasing use of foster care. Fox Harding has characterised much of the post-war period as reflecting a struggle between competing perspectives on child welfare ('laissez-faire and patriarchy', 'state paternalism and child protection', 'birth family and parents' rights' and 'children's rights and liberation') (Fox Harding, 1997). Although reality is inevitably more complex, it is helpful to view policy development in this way, with the 1975 Children Act reflecting the influence of state paternalism and child protection agendas and the 1989 Children Act more influenced by a parental rights and children's rights agenda.

It was certainly true that by the time of the Children Act 1989 the tide had swung against interventionism. There was also a strengthening of the long-developing trend towards foster care and away from institutional care. This was a response to a mixture of cost factors (residential care was and remains comparatively expensive) and ideological factors (a revived concern over the importance of family life). Finally, there was also a general decrease in numbers entering care around this time; from 92,000 in 1981 to 54,000 in 1998 (Hayden *et al.*, 1999, p. 36). Under the post-1997 New Labour governments, numbers rose steadily to 59,700 by 2002 (Department of Health, 2002a, p. 1).

This group of children and young people enter care for a wide variety of reasons. However, Table 5.1 shows that there is considerable overlap with the child protection system. Such links between the wider system of care for looked after children and increasing public and professional concern over child abuse came together dramatically in the 1990s through the State child abuse cases already mentioned and the consequent publication of a series of major reports on such abuse. The 'Pindown' inquiry (Levy and Kahan, 1991) in Staffordshire, the report on the activities of Frank Beck in Leicestershire (Kirkwood, 1993) and the investigation into widespread physical and sexual abuse in North Wales (Waterhouse, 2000) changed the terms of debate about the looked after system. Since the usual tensions between the privacy of the family and the rights of the child to protection from abuse (so striking and explosive in the Cleveland case: see Department of Health and Social Security, 1988) were absent here, there was little to prevent government from becoming significantly more interventionist in response. It duly became so. Nor was this rash of abuse inquiries a uniquely British phenomenon; similar institutional abuse scandals were emerging in other countries at the same time – primarily in Ireland, Canada and Australia (see Wolmar, 2000, pp. 206–216).

Table 5.1 Children looked after on 31 March 2002 by category of need

Reason for being looked after	Numbers	Percentage
Abuse or neglect	37,100	62
Family in acute stress	4,100	7
Absent parenting	4,300	7
Parent's illness or disability	3,700	6
Family dysfunction	6,200	10
Socially unacceptable behaviour	2,000	3
Disability	2,300	4
Total	59,700	100

Source: DoH, 2002a, p. 9.

What was often missing from the debate that emerged about how to respond to this problem, at least until the development of the QP initiative in 1998, was sufficient recognition of the extent to which prevailing conceptions of childhood compounded the vulnerability of children to abuse. Perceptions of looked after children, in particular, as either victims (of parental abuse and neglect) or villains (as youth offenders in practice or in training) did not encourage much stress on their agency, subjectivity or rights to participation in everyday decision-making. Given the relative isolation of many looked after children, any child protection process which regards such children primarily as vulnerable and in need of adult oversight is likely to fail; in these cases, the abuse came from those charged with such oversight. On the other hand, viewing such children as difficult, dangerous or out of control makes them less likely to be believed should they speak out about abuse; as the police themselves have acknowledged (Police Complaints Authority, 1993).

The representations and complaints procedure introduced by the 1989 Act (Section 26) had been a significant step forward in ensuring the development of adequate avenues for young people to be heard. There is a clear emphasis in Section 22 of the Act and in the relevant guidance (Department of Health, 1991b, p. 48) on the importance of children in care being consulted by local authorities before decisions are made about them. Moreover, the extensive discussion of complaints and representation procedures in the Guidance gives a high degree of prominence to making these processes accessible to children (Department of Health, 1991b, pp. 74–87). However, Wallis and Frost's investigations of the complaints procedure in practice (Wallis and Frost, 1998) concluded that it arose as much from protectionist instincts as from a concern over children's rights. For this reason, it failed to take sufficient account of the importance of information for children (the Act merely required that local authorities publicise their procedures 'as they consider appropriate') and of the need for a habit or culture of regular involvement by children in decision-making processes. This neglect seriously militated against the capacity to use, and the faith of children in, the complaints procedure. Moreover, others have questioned its 'independence' (Lyon, 1997).

Alongside problems of implementation, there were also problems of motivation. The prominence given by the 1989 Children Act to the rights of children had died down by the mid-1990s, amidst the fears of residential social workers, in particular, of the 'excessive' powers that it had given to young people (Berridge and Brodie, 1998, p. 134). Indeed, even some children in care appeared to view the 'rights' that they had been granted by the Act as something of a mixed blessing (Butler and Williamson, 1994, pp. 101–102). Nor was the profile of the voice of such young people helped by the collapse of the National Association of Young People in Care (NAYPIC) in 1994, the only independently run national group that was representing their views. Overall, the early 1990s saw some advances in ensuring that children were heard. However, since such advances took place within a paradigm of childhood vulnerability or irresponsibility rather than agency, their impact was limited.

Wider morale within the care system was also a problem. By the 1990s, going into care had increasingly come to be seen as a last resort and a symptom of failure. This was particularly so with respect to residential care. Whilst numbers in care had begun to rise again in the late 1990s, this rise was accounted for chiefly by an increase in the use of foster care; numbers in children's homes continued to decline. By March 2002, 66 per cent of looked after children in England were fostered while only 10 per cent were in children's homes. The rest were in a variety of other placements such as residential schools or with their own parents (Department of Health, 2002a, p. 6).

Quality Protects

Part of the New Labour government's response to the problems that we have been considering was to launch, in September 1998, the QP initiative (Department of Health, 1998b, pp. 54–56). This focused on a number of broad objectives with respect to services for children (including, but not restricted to, looked after children) and attached specific performance indicators to most of them. The main objectives relevant to looked after children were:

- ensuring secure attachment to appropriate carers;
- maximising life chances with regard to education, health and social care;
- enabling care leavers to participate socially and economically in society;
- the meaningful involvement of users and carers in planning services and tailoring individual packages of care;

- ensuring effective complaints mechanisms; and
- protection of children in regulated services from harm and poor care standards.

(Robbins, 2000, p. 105)

In order to make such measures concrete, a number of targets were produced which local authorities had to report on to central government. These included the following: reducing the numbers of looked after children experiencing three or more placement moves a year; reducing the numbers of looked after children with final warnings, reprimands or convictions; increasing the percentage of children having routine immunisations completed and yearly dental checks and health assessments; increasing the numbers of children adopted compared to those who had been in care for 6 months or more; reducing the percentages of children who had missed more than 25 days schooling in the previous year; and, finally, increasing the percentage in care for 4 years who were currently in a foster placement where they had been for at least 2 years. Such measures were designed to ratchet up performance with respect to both the stability of children and their basic care.

As with many apparently new policy developments, this one sought to build on already existing practice. For example, the use of Action and Assessment Records – which sought to measure the well-being of children along a number of different developmental dimensions such as health care, education, social relationships and self-care skills – had spread to 92 per cent of local authorities by 1997 (House of Commons Health Select Committee, 1998, p. xxii) and was lauded in the *Modernising Social Services'* White Paper (Department of Health, 1998a, p. 56). Much of the government's QP initiative can be seen as a transfer of this approach from the individualistic, child-focused level of monitoring onto the broader canvas of public policy.

Other key features of the programme included the greater involvement of local councillors in implementing the underlying philosophy of 'corporate parenting' and an enhanced performance measurement and inspection regime. Extra money was provided for the achievement of improvements in the above areas (£885m over 5 years, from 1999 to 2004) on the basis of a detailed annual 'Management Action Plan' (MAP) produced by each local authority. Although QP was in part a comprehensive attempt to address the full range of major problems already identified with respect to looked after children, two particular areas – educational achievement and leaving care provision – were singled out for extra attention.

The education of looked after children

Emphasis on improving educational performance was a particularly prominent feature of ministerial statements on QP. This subject had gained a high profile in the 1990s due to an increasing body of research, a Department of Health and Department for Education and Employment joint circular (1994) and a joint SSI/ OFSTED investigation (1995) (see Goddard, 2000). However, there was a widespread acceptance by the late 1990s that educational disaffection and low achievement continued to be a major problem (House of Commons Education and Employment Select Committee, 1998, p. vii; House of Commons Health Select Committee, 1998, pp. lxi–lxvii). A consensus on the need to address this problem resulted in separate and detailed guidance on the subject, issued jointly by the Department for Education and Employment and the Department of Health (Department of Health and Department for Education and Employment, 2000). This guidance focused on both raising the priority of educational achievement for looked after children within social services and improving co-operation between social services departments and local education providers. It introduced the appointment of designated teachers within schools to ensure action for looked after children; for example, that each child had the mandatory Personal Education Plan. It also prioritised educational continuity during placement moves by placing time limits on educational gaps that might occur between such moves. All of this was designed to achieve, in the first instance, what some regarded as a woefully unambitious target, as part of the Department of Health's Performance Assessment Framework:

> improve the educational attainment of children looked after, by increasing to at least 50% by 2001 the proportion of children leaving care at 16 or later with a GCSE or GNVQ qualification; and to 75% by 2003 (Department of Health, 2000c, p. 51).

In response to the valid criticism from many quarters that one GCSE was virtually useless in the employment and education markets, a further target was introduced: increasing to 15 per cent by 2003/2004 the proportion of care leavers aged over 16 with 5 GCSEs grades A–C (Department of Health, 2003a).

Leaving care

The area of leaving care provision has seen significant policy development through the passage of the Children (Leaving Care) Act 2000. This Act set out to remedy perceived deficiencies in the 1989 Children Act – primarily Section 24 of that Act. These deficiencies had been analysed by a number of academic and official sources during the 1990s (see Goddard, 2001). The central problem with Section 24 was that its more supportive features with respect to care leavers were introduced as powers rather than duties. Also, significant problems arose from its context. First, it was implemented at a time of considerable financial constraint on local authorities and of high youth unemployment. Secondly, other policy developments counteracted its objectives; for example, benefit rates and entitlements had already been reduced for young people under the age of 25 by the Social Security Acts of 1986 and 1988, and the Housing Act 1996 had removed the capacity of local authorities to provide priority status for care leavers.

By the late 1990s, there was general official acknowledgement of the need for further action (Utting, 1997, pp. 91–93; Social Services Inspectorate, 1997). The Children (Leaving Care) Act 2000 introduced a number of developments designed to improve the level and length of support available to care leavers. These developments included a 'needs assessment' and a 'pathway plan' by the age of 16, to take young people through the transition to independence up to and beyond the age of 21. The implementation of this plan is overseen by a 'personal adviser' for the young person during this time. A controversial feature of the Act was the removal of entitlement to means-tested benefits for most care leavers between the ages of 16 and 18. Local social services departments would now provide such financial support. Further extensions of support included the authority that last looked after the young person retaining responsibility for after-care support – even if the young person moves from the local area – a duty of social services departments to keep in touch with these young people up to, at least, the age of 21 and, finally, post-care assistance with education and training, including vacation accommodation for those in higher education who require it (First Key, 2001). Alongside the Act, other measures were also designed to assist care leavers, either directly or through more general social policy changes. The Housing Act 2002, for example, compels local authorities to carry out a review of homelessness in their area and to develop a strategy to respond to it in co-operation with local statutory agencies.

Parenting and 'corporate parenting'

Concepts of 'good parenting' are used in quite distinctive ways within this field. 'Corporate parenting' – state paternalism for the new millennium – builds on the implications for local authorities of being 'in loco parentis' in respect of children for whom they care. Both QP and the Children (Leaving Care) Act 2000 attempt to apply flesh to the bones, with respect to local authorities, of the necessarily vague definition of this concept of 'parental responsibility' as being 'the collection of duties, rights and authority which a parent has in respect of his child' (Department of Health, 1989, p. 1). With respect to the QP programme, the application of this concept also requires local authorities to use their housing, leisure and other resources to support the work of their social services departments (Department of Health, 1998a). This paternalistic oversight model contains a key role for local councillors (Smith, in Robbins, 2001, p. 1). The focus is on inter-agency working as a way of bringing all of the local authority's resources (such as education, leisure and housing) into play.

The Act strengthens this formulation with a conception of what it means to take account of the gradual and lengthy process of transition to independence by providing, as the regulations and guidance put it, 'the support that a good parent might be expected to give' (Department of Health, 2001c, p. 27). Thus, one can see in the 'needs assessment' a parallel to the discussions about the future that many parents engage in with their children prior to sixth-form education. Similarly, the changes to the benefit system for 16–18-year-olds are an attempt to preserve the parental purse strings in the way that they are maintained for most young people of that age. This particular measure was introduced to counteract a growing tendency for young people to leave the care system at the age of 16. The Department of Health and others had argued that this resulted from a 'perverse financial incentive' for local authorities to help or encourage young people to leave care – at which point, the central government benefits system would pick up the living costs of these young people (Department of Health, 1999b, p. 12; House of Commons Health Select Committee, 1998, p. lxviii). Finally, the flexibility of the Pathway Plan, the regular contact from the Personal Adviser, and the potential for support with training and with accommodation during university vacations all attempt to replicate a model of good parenting.

At the time, this approach did raise some concerns about the civil liberties implications of both state monitoring of the lives of young people beyond the age of 18 (Hansard, 21 June 2000, col. 371) and the removal of social security benefits for most care leavers between the ages of 16 and 18 (Calder, 2000, pp. 11–13). However, in support of a more paternalistic approach one can argue that the reason for past failure is that an individualistic, rights-based approach to transitions to independence is not appropriate for this group of young people in the absence of other support. Indeed, just as important as the level of financial support available (which must be 'above benefit levels', according to the Act's subsequent Guidance) is the element of compulsion on local authorities and young people to maintain their relationship with each other until at least age 18 and the compulsion on local authorities to go on doing this beyond 18. Studies of care leavers (for example, Stein and Carey, 1986; Lynes and Goddard, 1995) had repeatedly demonstrated that many care leavers felt an acute and personal sense of abandonment by local authorities at this transition stage in their lives, even in cases where their relationship with social services had been difficult. Given that, as we know, young people now increasingly leave home in their early to mid-twenties on average (Jones, 1995; Coleman and Schofield, 2001, p. 11), a genuine replication of parental responsibility is a tall order. The Act itself, needless to say, does not meet such grand objectives.

Children, parents and the state

Alongside developments in state paternalism, there have also been developments in the areas of children's rights, parental rights and support for parenting models. Each of these has its own rationale, but they also create tensions between each other.

The single biggest consequence of the abuse inquiry reports noted above was to increase recognition of the importance of consulting children in care in order to protect them. These circumstances made it possible for a paternalistic, child protection agenda and a children's rights approach to fruitfully coincide. Much of the investigation of these scandals emphasised – either explicitly or implicitly – the importance of the user's voice in preventing abuse.

It is therefore not surprising that both the QP initiative and the Children (Leaving Care) Act 2000 emphasised even more strongly than the Children Act 1989 the right of young people to be involved in decision-making about their lives. The QP initiative developed this line of thinking into the funding of a national pressure group ('A National Voice'), run by and for such young people, to replace NAYPIC. Also, Objective Eight of QP seeks to improve the involvement of young people in the care process in three ways:

1. involvement in the planning and review of services;
2. involvement in decision-making with respect to individual care;
3. the operation of effective complaints mechanisms.

Subsequently, the government's response to the Waterhouse Report (Department of Health, 2000d) reiterated the importance of changing attitudes on this issue within the looked after system through a range of measures. These included training for local authority elected councillors and front-line staff and, through the Adoption and Children Act 2002, a requirement on local authorities to provide an advocacy service to children wishing to make representations about the services provided for them (Lind, 2003). The central rationale is protection from abuse, highlighting 'the constant need for vigilance, of the need to ensure that children being looked after can always talk freely about their concerns and worries' (Department of Health, 2000d, p. 61). It is important to note this rationale, since it is not at all clear that this focus on the voices of children would have emerged in the absence of the abuse inquiries.

A rationale for the involvement of parents in decision-making is less clear-cut, except insofar as the government repeats the basic reasoning of the 1989 Children Act on the importance of working in partnership with families. With respect to looked after children and care leavers, this relates to involvement in decision-making where appropriate and, most importantly, maintaining contact (Department of Health, 2000c). Notwithstanding the presentation of the 1989 Children Act as a 'Children's Charter' in the early 1990s, it is also clear that it represented a partial victory for those who sought to retain family involvement in the lives of looked after children (particularly as a countervailing power to the discretion of professionals) (Fox Harding, 1997, pp. 182–185). Subsequent guidance on the Act emphasised the importance of family involvement both with respect to child protection processes (Ryan, 1999, pp. 71–73) and with respect to contact with, and the participation of, the families of children who are looked after.

However, in this particular context the government's approach was to shift the emphasis on parenting and families away from birth families and towards substitute families. Adoption was promoted with increasing vigour by the 1997–2001 government and this resulted in an Adoption and Children Act in 2002. This Act speeds up UK adoption processes and tightens up arrangements for overseas adoptions, but it also contains a strong emphasis on improving the levels of adoption from care (Labour Party, 2001, p. 28; Department of Health, 2000b). One background factor suggesting that there was scope for expansion in this area, notwithstanding the various social and cultural factors involved, was that the number of adoptions had dropped to just over 5000 in the year 2000 – a quarter of the number 30 years earlier (Matheson and Babb, 2002, p. 50). Consequently, the percentage of children from within the care system being put forward for adoption had risen during the early 1990s, from 3 per cent in 1991 to 4.5 per cent in 1996 (House of Commons Health Select Committee, 1998, p. xxxvi). The House of Commons Health Select Committee report on looked after children did not go so far as to explicitly recommend a continued increase, but its criticism of local authorities for failing 'to take adoption sufficiently seriously as an option' (House of Commons Health Select Committee, 1998, p. xxxviii), and for unnecessary delays, left little room for any other interpretation. Alongside the 2002 Act, New Labour introduced an Adoption and Permanence Taskforce to promote good practice, an Adoption Register for England to bring together adopters and potential adoptees, and National Adoption Standards. The Act itself legally compelled, via Section 22, local authorities to make early preparation for adoption where care plans were already directed towards that end (Lind, 2003). Such activity produced results, with the number of looked after children freed for adoption rising by 58 per cent between 1998 and 2002 and with 3600 being placed for adoption by 31 March 2002, up 5 per cent on the previous year (Department of Health, 2002b).

This preference for adoption highlights one of the more worrying trends in New Labour's approach. In 1997, the Utting Report highlighted the importance of restoring and developing a healthy residential sector. It noted what other research has found; that many young people prefer residential care to fostering. New Labour's fondness for promoting the family model, whether through fostering or adoption, is of course cheaper than residential care. However, it also limits choice. The development of both fostering and adoption is encouraged by government targets but, while 'choice' is encouraged by government, the number of children's home places has continued to decline, from 6600 in 1998 to 6000 in 2002 (Department of Health, 2002a), even as numbers in care generally have risen. Moreover, well over a third of such placements are outside the local authority boundary. Residential care can offer a viable long-term solution for many young people, particularly those who experience difficulties in foster care (Frost, et al., 1999). In this instance, however, New Labour's response to the perceived problems of the past appears to have produced a rather narrow-minded assessment of future options.

Control, regulation and targeting

With respect to the involvement of the State with those young people who have entered the care system, the lessons of the 1990s were contradictory. On the one hand, the evident failures in the areas of protection from abuse and outcomes more generally provided encouragement to those who favoured avoidance of the use of the care system wherever possible. However, such failures also encouraged greater state involvement for those young people who remained within the care system. One feature of such involvement was a significantly enhanced regulation and inspection regime with regard to looked after children. This was a response not only to poor outcomes, but also to management problems. Social Services Inspectorate reports and joint reviews had repeatedly shown that the quality of children's services was inconsistent – both within and between local authorities (see Social Services Inspectorate, 1997, 1998a,b; Social Services Inspectorate/OFSTED, 1995). The response of New Labour's first Health Secretary, Frank Dobson, was at one with the government's approach across the public sector – to provide extra resources but to tie those resources very specifically to the meeting of centrally set and monitored targets and standards. The alteration of the regulatory regime for looked after children took place in the context of a wider reorganisation of the social services system more generally. The Care Standards Act 2000 introduced an independent regulatory system that superseded the invidious position in which the local authority has been both the purchaser and the inspector of some services. In 2002, a National Care Standards Commission (NCSC), with supplementary regional and area structures, took responsibility for the registration and inspection of services in England (separate, though similar, bodies were established in Scotland and Wales). Its remit included all children's homes, including those run by local authorities and independent fostering agencies, residential family centres, independent and local authority fostering services, and boarding schools (previously not covered by the Department of Health regulatory regime).

Working for the Commission was a Children's Rights Director with a remit to, among other things:

> ensure that the Commission safeguards and promotes the rights and welfare of children who are provided with regulated children's services and that the views of children placed in these facilities and services are given due weight by the NCSC in that regulatory task (National Care Standards Commission, 2002, p. 11).

As with QP and the Children (Leaving Care) Act, this represents a move to apply nationally the lessons of local best practice. The growth in the number of Children's Rights Officers employed by local authorities was a particularly bright spot in policy towards looked after children during the 1990s. The government, learning lessons from the scale of abuse uncovered by the enquiries already mentioned, saw fit to lift this practice onto a national plane. The same approach underpinned the issuing of 'National Minimum Standards' by the Commission. Two sets of standards are of particular relevance to this chapter, those for fostering services and those for children's homes. The latter covered a wide range of areas including both quality of care (privacy arrangements, action on bullying) and environmental concerns (bathing facilities, bedrooms). The fostering standards place much less stress on such matters of daily care and much more on the adequate training, recruitment and supervision of foster carers.

Looked after children: reforms and practice

With respect to the impact of this strategy, the early evidence was mixed. The Department of Health's annual evaluations of local authority MAPs and of relevant statistical data (for example, Robbins, 2001) suggest improvement in some of the areas that government has required them to focus on. This includes improvement in the stability of short-term foster placements, with the numbers of children moved more than three times a year kept significantly below the 16 per cent target. Other areas also showed improvement, with more reviews taking place on time, reduced exclusions from school and absence rates and improved involvement of young people in decision-making. Areas with low or no improvement included reducing the numbers of children becoming involved in the criminal justice system, ensuring regular health care attention and improving accessibility to complaints procedures. A lot of developments, such as mental health support systems through Children and Adolescent Mental Health Services (CAMHS), still appeared to be at the planning stages. MAPs will have disappeared in 2004 as the QP programme is 'mainstreamed' through assessment by the social services inspectorate and the removal of a ring-fenced budget. Given the slow progress thus far, there must be doubts as to whether such improvements will be sustained.

On the education front, progress has also been slow. More specifically, the targets on educational performance were not achieved by local authorities. The percentage of children leaving care with one GCSE or GNVQ rose through 2000 to 2002 from 31 to 41 per cent. The figures for children achieving five or more GCSEs at grades A–C fared even worse. In the non-care population, 50 per cent of children now achieve this threshold. For care leavers, however, the numbers merely rose from 4 per cent in 2000 to 5 per cent in 2002 (Department of Health, 2003a). With no prospect at all of hitting the existing targets, the government adopted the time-honoured strategy of changing the targets. These became that 90 per cent of care leavers should have sat (not necessarily passed) a GCSE exam by 2006 and that 15 per cent should have passed five or more GCSEs by 2006. The government also instituted an investigation into the subject through the Social Exclusion Unit (Smith, 2002), which became part of the preparation of the 2003 'Children at Risk' Green Paper. This depressing downscaling of the government's ambitions in this area has significant implications, of course, for the numbers of care leavers going on to university. No reliable figures are available on this, but all estimates suggest that it is extremely low, in the region of 1–2 per cent (Jackson *et al.*, 2003). On leaving care support, there is more hopeful evidence. QP had included performance measures in this area, such as keeping in touch with young people after they leave care and the percentages in training, employment or education. Councils remained in touch with 75 per cent of care leavers on or near their nineteenth birthday. This might seem a small achievement, but given what we know from past research about how quickly young people disappear from local authority sight, it represents significant progress. With respect to the specific target of the percentage of 19-year-old care leavers in education, training or employment (it should be 60 per cent of that of their non-care peers by 2003/2004), the figure of 46 per cent compares to 86 per cent of their non-care peers (Department of Health, 2003a). However it is difficult to assess the meaning of this figure since it is the first time that such data has been available.

An exploratory assessment of the Act, produced a year after the Act's implementation, suggested evidence of improvement in some areas and problems in others (see Roberts Centre, 2003). On the positive side, the new financial arrangements appeared to be working more smoothly than many anticipated, with many care leavers being paid directly into their bank accounts. Also, the collection of leaving care data is providing a much more robust dataset with which to plan services. There is also evidence of widespread, if variable, involvement of young people in planning and decision-making. On the less positive side, some personal advisers appear to be developing a bureaucratic interpretation of their role rather than a supportive and advisory one. Also, some young people have complained of the inflexibility of pathway plans. Finally, while there appears to have been a slight decline in young people leaving care before the age of 18, there are still obstacles to them remaining in caring, supportive environments (for example, with their foster carers) beyond that age. Other research also suggests a mixed picture. Broad's survey of 52 leaving-care teams points to improvements in planning, education and training, staffing and assessing young people's finances. In particular, it noted that the numbers going into post-16 education had risen from 17.5 per cent in 1998 to 31 per cent by 2003. However, it notes continued problems in areas such as health, dealing with disability and early discharge from care (Broad, 2003).

Discussion

Given the plethora of initiatives in recent years, one can accuse the New Labour government of seeking to counteract what it sees as local authority inertia with central government hyperactivity. There has certainly been a strong state paternalist approach in this policy field, prompted in part by the centrality of looked after children to the government's social investment strategy. As we have seen, this is not antithetical to a children's rights approach and the government has sought to act on participation and involvement rights through the participation of looked after children as an objective under QP and their involvement in leaving care planning under the Children (Leaving Care) Act. On the other hand, the top-down bias in favour of adoption and fostering and against residential care, intended or otherwise, is inconsistent with this participatory agenda and places limitations on the genuineness of choices available to some young people.

The effectiveness of the strategy has been mixed. Whether the addiction to targets has served looked after children better than a simpler strategy of providing local authorities with more money and more discretion is an argument that applies equally well to the rest of New Labour's approach in the public sector. With respect to education, however, it is surely doubtful whether such progress as has been achieved would have occurred without the apparatus of QP. There is considerable evidence of a low priority being given to education within local authorities (see Goddard, 2000). Such problems with past local authority performance are not always sufficiently recognised by critics of the government's approach. Munro, for example, in a generally admirable discussion of the views of looked after children about their involvement in decision-making (Munro, 2001), suggests that the target-setting of QP might inhibit the discretion of social workers and local authorities who wish to respond to children's wishes. This underplays both the importance of Objective Eight (involving young people) to the QP initiative and also the nature of the problems that QP is attempting to address. Her complaint about the shift of social workers away from working on emotional and behavioural problems reflects a faith in qualitative work and measures which, on the basis of the quantitative indicators which led to QP, is unjustified.

The government's focus on increasing educational achievement, developing leisure interests and otherwise seeking to compel local authorities to build up the resources of young people through education is an important and neglected strategy. It accords with what some writers in this field have been arguing for some time is central to change; building up the independent resourcefulness and resilience of looked after children (Gilligan, 1997, 2000; Jackson, 1998). In this context, a social investment focus on education and employment as the primary route out of disadvantage is a wholly welcome one. It certainly is paternalism by the State, but primarily paternalism over local authorities; removing their discretion in some contexts on the grounds that too many of them have signally failed to use it well in the past with respect to the long-term interests of looked after children.

Conclusion

Government's commitment to change and improvement in this area appears genuine and long-term. It has at least outlasted their first term of government. The picture is mixed, but it is at least progressive. For example, the appointment of Margaret Hodge as the first Minister for Children and Young People in 2003 raised unease due to her stewardship of Islington Council in the 1980s when abuse allegations emerged. Her subsequent description of a successful care leaver as 'extremely disturbed', in an attempt to stop a BBC investigation into her work in Islington, confirmed such unease. Also on the negative side is the relative down-playing of looked after children within the extremely broad agenda of the 2003 Green Paper on 'children at risk' (Chief Secretary to the Treasury, 2003). On the positive side, the Green Paper's proposal of creating a Director of Children's Services to link local authority social services and education may enhance the educational agenda for looked after children. Similarly, the commitment to introduce measurement of the performance of care leavers in higher education, announced in the 2003 Social Exclusion Unit report on this subject (Social Exclusion Unit, 2003), will help to maintain the profile of this subject. This focus on education should not be surprising given, as we set out at the start, the centrality of looked after children and care leavers to initial discussions of the social exclusion of children and young people and their clear location at the heart of a social investment model of child welfare. Some have criticised the shift of New Labour's focus from inequality to social exclusion (Callinicos, 2001). The interest in social investment opportunities has led to a further narrowing of the focus. However, for looked after children these shifts have clearly brought advantages. By rendering them more visible, it has produced a more concentrated set of policy responses than might otherwise have been forthcoming. Alongside the recipients of 'Sure Start' and families in poverty, they have been amongst the main beneficiaries of a social investment strategy for child welfare policy.

CHAPTER 6

Youth Justice

Introduction

This chapter considers recent developments in policy and practice with respect to young offenders between the ages of 10 and 17 in England (Scotland's youth justice system is significantly different). These developments also apply to Wales, since this remains one policy area in which central government does not have a separate policy approach solely for England. Developing youth justice policies for children in this category clearly presents distinctive challenges to any government, raising issues of care and punishment in a context that generates considerable public emotion and media attention and hence presents significant political risks. One way in which this chapter differs from most others in this volume is that the Children Act 1989 is conspicuous by its absence. This alone says much, as we shall see, about the UK government's approach in this field.

Whilst focusing on developments in the 1990s, particularly those since 1997, the chapter begins by placing such developments in a wider historical context. It is important to do this, since the subject of youth justice has periodically been extremely prominent in political and media discussion over many decades in the UK – much more so than most of the other areas of policy towards children and young people that we are considering. For this reason, past debates and policy developments strongly influence contemporary positions. More than in any other policy area in this book, New Labour's approach to youth justice cannot be understood outside of its perception of the political costs of its previous policies in this field and in the field of criminal justice policy more generally.

With respect to the post-1997 changes, we are discussing a particularly fertile period. The Crime and Disorder Act 1998 included a number of major policy initiatives on youth justice. It was followed only a year later by the Youth Justice and Criminal Evidence Act 1999, the most significant innovation of which was the Referral Order. We consider these and other developments in the light of wider policy objectives. This enables us to recognise the problematic links between New Labour's approach to young offenders and the politics of the 'Third Way':

> The Third Way has moved beyond the old divide between social or individual responsibility. Citizens are responsible for their own actions, but we acknowledge and deal with the conditions in which crime breeds, like family breakdown, drug abuse and social exclusion (Blair, 1998, p. 12).

In the context of this 'Third Way', we are here examining the 'responsibilities' (to obey the law) that go with the 'rights' (to services and social protection) accorded to young people in other contexts. This constitutes another element in New Labour's social investment strategy; the use of control to ensure wider compliance with market-friendly child welfare, education, and labour market policies. Young people who have broken the law are faced with a renewed emphasis on personal responsibility, whilst most support is reserved for young people who have accepted their responsibilities to obey the law. This veers closely towards (though does not quite become) a 'social contract' model of welfare, in which benefits are conditional upon behaviour; a model which has been applied by New Labour more clearly elsewhere, such as in the social security system through the New Deal for young people. Such an approach to youth justice is an attempt to respond to perceived public anxieties on youth crime whilst implying a proactive approach to social problems that could appeal to those on the political left by linking social order with social justice (Blair, 1996). This dualism echoed Margaret Thatcher's similarly successful linking of the concepts of the 'free economy' and the 'strong state' during the 1980s (Gamble, 1988).

Crime by young people is such a central feature of policy debate on crime more generally because it contributes so much to the crime total. In the mid-1990s, the Audit Commission noted that two out of every five offenders were under the age of 21 and one in four was under the age of 18 (Audit Commission, 1996, p. 5). It is this latter group of young offenders that we are concerned with here. More specifically, we are concerned with:

1. children between the ages of 10 and 14 who have committed a crime (and who cannot usually be tried for indictment, except when charged with homicide); and

2. children between the ages of 14 and 17 (who can be so charged, depending on the seriousness of the offence and/or the age of any co-defendants).

Most of these young offenders will be tried summarily at a Magistrates or Youth Court and, rather than imprisonment, face detention in a young offender institution for those cases where detention is required but which fall short of homicide. Since the Criminal Justice and Public Order Act of 1994, it has also been possible to sentence an offender aged 12–14 to custody. Following the 1998 Act, young offenders became eligible for a new generic custodial sentence for serious offenders between the ages of 12 and 18, the Detention and Training Order (under the Act, the Home Secretary also holds reserve powers to apply custody to children as young as 10, if necessary). However, a wide range of alternative sentences – such as community service, probation, fines, supervision orders and attendance at an attendance centre – have long been available.

From Old to New Labour on youth justice

Historically, criminal justice policy has been an under-researched area of Labour Party policy change. It was conspicuous by its absence from many reviews of developments in Labour public policy fields until recent years. Since the mid-1990s, this neglect has been rectified (for example, Coates and Lawler, 2000; Seldon, 2001; Charman and Savage, 2002). However, the chief reason for this relative historical neglect is that Labour's own interest in this subject is itself comparatively recent: the Labour Party's first national conference debates on crime or criminal justice did not take place until 1978 and 1981. Meanwhile, the Conservatives had been debating the subject almost annually since the mid-1950s.

The Conservative interest from the mid-1950s onwards reflected the development of a significant crime wave, as measured in official statistics. Recorded crime rose by only 5 per cent in the decade following the end of the Second World War. However, the major rises from 1957 onwards (121 per cent between 1957 and 1967 and doubling again in the decade after that) became a major political issue. While the rate of increase slowed from the late 1970s to the early 1990s, 'recorded crime was still 50% higher in 1987 than a decade earlier' (Hood and Roddam, 2000, p. 680). It was not until the mid-1990s (1993 for recorded crime and 1995 for victimisation, as measured by the British Crime Survey [BCS]) that crime rates began to fall. The problem of crime that developed from the late 1950s onwards was out of all proportion to that of previous decades of the twentieth century: from 1900 to 1957, crime figures rose from 77,934 to 545,562; from then until 1997 they rose to 4,460,629 (Hood and Roddam, 2000, pp. 682–683).

The reform-minded approaches of Conservative Home Secretary (1957–1962) R. A. Butler and of Labour's influential Longford Report (1964) are particularly illustrative of a new politics of affluence in which politicians and intellectuals sought to come to terms with the growth of crime in the context of a developing welfare state and continued economic growth. One central theme of this period might be characterised as the politics of failure, in which more or less continual growth in recorded crime figures led to alternating bouts of authoritarian and welfare-based reform, as each approach was perceived to have failed by its opponents.

Thus it was that Labour's 1969 Children and Young Persons Act became a source of irritation to Conservatives throughout the 1970s. The most significant – and contentious – feature of that Act was the replacement of the specific sentencing powers of magistrates with the power to issue a Care Order. Through placing a child in the care of a local authority, who were then to provide the most appropriate (that is, beneficial for the child) placement, this aimed to funnel young offenders away from the youth justice system and into the child care system. Such a blurring of the boundaries between the two systems was attacked vigorously by some, both at the time and in subsequent years (see *Parliamentary Debates*, 11.3.69).

Support for such a strongly interventionist approach had declined markedly by the late 1970s, after rising numbers of children had been brought into the new welfare/justice framework with what appeared to be little good effect (Goldson, 2000). The 1970s, split equally between the Conservatives (1970–1974 and 1979 onwards) and Labour (1974–1979), was a period of significant increase in the incarceration of young offenders under both administrations. For example, the numbers of 14–17-year-olds entering detention centres rose from 1404 in 1965 to 5757 by 1977 (Pitts, 1988, p. 19). Such increases in custody were not related to increases in youth crime but reflected a greater use of custody by the courts, with some speculation that this was in part the response of magistrates to the 1969 Act; seeking to remove serious offenders from the hands of social workers (Pitts, 1988, pp. 19–22). This increase occurred notwithstanding initiatives by the Heath government (through measures such as Community Service Orders in the 1972 Criminal Justice Act) and the Wilson and Callaghan governments (through the promotion of 'Intermediate Treatment') to develop 'community' alternatives. When in power from 1979, the Conservatives sought to reduce the social welfare features of the youth justice system. William Whitelaw, Home Secretary in the first Thatcher government, introduced the flawed 'short, sharp shock' experiment, designed to restore Detention Centres to their previously more punitive regime. Also, via the 1982 Criminal Justice Act, he amended the 1969 Act both to give courts greater powers to impose conditions on Care Orders and to tighten up Supervision Orders. Throughout much of the 1980s and 1990s, youth justice was part of the symbolic rhetoric of Conservative governments as they sought to establish a mandate for a more authoritarian approach to social policy in general. However, under successive Home Secretaries in the early 1980s and into the 1990s, strong rhetoric was combined with repeated moves to restrict custody of young offenders and to develop non-custodial alternatives. In part, the Conservatives were carrying forward the policy of 'bifurcation' – increased use of community sentences for less serious offences, along with harsher sentences for more serious offences – that had been initiated by the Heath government. This theme carried through the 1982 Criminal Justice Act, the 1988 Criminal Justice Act and the 1991 Criminal Justice Act.

On the other hand, the problem of continually rising recorded crime during most of this period led to continued pressure on governments to find new ways of addressing the issue. The early 1990s had begun with a continuation of the greater liberalism in policy of the late 1980s. The Criminal Justice Act 1991 exemplified this, seeking to shift sentencing away from penal sanctions and towards 'punishment in the community'. Problems with the Act, particularly with anomalies in the use of unit fines, led to some backtracking by Kenneth Clarke in 1993. Also, Clarke toughened up in relation to young offenders, proposing new secure training centres for 12–14-year-olds. The key background problem for the Conservatives, of the continually rising crime rate, had left them electorally exposed on the issue, even while their approach of minimising custody for young offenders was supported by both right and left; leading to the 1980s being viewed by some as a very positive period in youth justice policy (for example, Goldson, 2002). The increased use of custody in the 1990s, leading to a doubling of the numbers of 15–17-year-olds in custody between June 1993 and June 1998, was partly an attempt to reduce that political exposure.

Meanwhile, successive Labour Shadow Home Secretaries in the 1980s, Roy Hattersley and Gerald Kaufman, had begun to develop a twin-track strategy of remaining concerned with what they saw as the social roots of crime but becoming less concerned with the rights and conditions of offenders. Tony Blair and Jack Straw took this approach much further. Blair's appointment as Shadow Home Secretary in 1992 was important because of his appreciation of the electoral salience of criminal justice policy and his consequent willingness to break new ground on the issue within the Labour Party. It was his willingness to lead from the front on this subject that helped to secure him the Labour leadership in 1994 and which subsequently became a key feature of his policy agenda (see Blair, 1996, pp. 244–248; Rentoul, 2001, pp. 192–201). Also important was the murder of the 6-year-old James Bulger in February 1993 by two 10-year-old boys on Merseyside, an event which prompted considerable national debate on the supervision and control of children (see also Chapter 4). These factors, combined with the Major government's 'back to basics' campaign – designed to shore up its insecure political and electoral position – provided favourable conditions for an authoritarian refocusing of youth justice policy by both parties. As a result, the 1993 Criminal Justice Act and the 1994 Criminal Justice and Public Order Act introduced a much tougher approach (reflected, in the case of the latter, in the introduction of the secure training centres for 12–14-year-olds that had been promoted by Kenneth Clarke).

For the New Labour project, it was also significant that the BCSs of 1992 and 1994 demonstrated that specific geographic areas – primarily working class areas – suffered exceptionally high crime rates. The latter, for example, showed that 'inner-city renters' were five times more likely to be victims of burglary than 'rural owner-occupiers'. Social groups that were particular objects of concern for New Labour, such as African-Caribbean communities and single adults with children, were found to be particularly susceptible to burglary and to thefts involving vehicles (Home Office, 1995, p. 11). A subsequent qualitative analysis of the 1998 BCS data reinforced such findings (Maguire and Kynch, 2000, pp. 4–5). Data of this kind strengthened the arguments of 'new left realists', who sought to change traditional Labour thinking about the class-based nature of criminal justice policy, from seeing criminals as working class victims to seeing them as victimisers of the working class. After 1993, Blair and then (from 1994) Jack Straw sought to keep pace with the new Conservative Home Secretary, Michael Howard. This was not always easy, as Howard moved the Conservatives in an increasingly punitive direction based on the premise that 'prison works' (Benyon and Edwards, 1997). However, Straw proved so adept at following Howard that opposition to Conservative proposals increasingly tended to come from senior judges and from the House of Lords (including former Conservative Home Secretaries).

New Labour's approach proved electorally successful. From being significantly behind the Conservatives in 1979, in respect of opinion poll findings on which party had the best approach to crime, they had overtaken the Conservatives by 1995 (Peel, 1997, pp. 97–98). The party was responding to the perceived authoritarianism of its own voters and there was certainly evidence to suggest that such perceptions had some substance. For example, it is worth noting that support for capital punishment had increased – for all age categories – between 1963 and 1987 and has always been highest amongst manual working class voters (Crewe *et al.*, 1991, pp. 408–409). With respect to youth justice in particular, Labour's growing confidence in the appeal of its approach is evident in the contrast between the General Election manifestos of 1987 and 1992, which do not mention the subject (Labour Party, 1987, 1992), and the election manifesto for 1997, which contained the following commitments:

- To half the time it takes from arrest to sentencing.
- To replace repeat cautions with a single final warning.
- To develop area-based 'Youth Offending Teams'.
- To streamline Youth Courts.
- To introduce 'parental responsibility orders' in order to make parents deal with their children's misbehaviour.
- 'Zero tolerance' of petty crime by young offenders.

(Labour Party, 1997, pp. 22–23)[1]

This strong emphasis on youth crime coincided with strong public concern over this subject. For example, the performance of Youth Courts was regarded as 'poor' or 'very poor' by almost half of 1998 BCS respondents (Home Office, 2000, p. 17) and three quarters thought that the treatment of young offenders by the courts was too lenient (Home Office, 2000, p. 18). There was also concern over the proportion of crimes committed by young people and the perceived increase in the numbers of young offenders. However, while New Labour was clearly responding to such perceptions, it ignored the more important underlying reality that the public was wrong on both counts; public perceptions significantly overestimated the percentage of crime committed by young people and the numbers of young offenders remained stable between 1995 and 1997 (Home Office, 2000, pp. 11–14). On the other hand, perceptions mattered greatly to a party that was as desperate for votes as Labour was by 1997, and law and order was a significant issue during the election; it was third in terms of press coverage and had become more important to voters between 1992 and 1997 (King *et al.*, 1998, pp. 132, 194).

Youth justice and the Crime and Disorder Act 1998

> I suspect that the two major political parties are now closer together on law and order issues than at any time in the past 20 years (Edward Leigh MP, Hansard, 8 April 1998, col. 420).

Following the 1997 General Election, Jack Straw quickly issued three separate consultation papers on youth justice. In the first of these, Straw was emphatic in his focus on individual responsibility:

> Young people who commit crime must face up to the consequences of their actions for themselves and for others and must take responsibility for their actions…When young people offend, the response of the youth justice system should be rapid, consistent and effective. No young person should be allowed to feel that he or she can offend with impunity (Home Office, 1997a, pp. 2–3).

Labour's approach sought to overcome – or ignore, depending on one's perspective – previously existing tensions between the welfare and control of young people by making them the responsibility of separate arms of government. This is evident from the subsequent White Paper on youth crime. After outlining a range of punitive measures, the White Paper makes clear the links between the youth justice strategy and wider measures to tackle social exclusion in areas such as unemployment, truancy and the provision of nursery education (see Home Office, 1997b, p. 10). The problem with this presentation of policy as though it is concerned with both welfare and control is the sleight-of-hand involved; whilst previous approaches sought to balance welfare and control with respect to young offenders, the new approach separates them out and applies them to *different* groups of young people; non-offenders and offenders respectively.

Therefore, while there is a much wider context within which New Labour's punitive measures must be cast, the Act itself was intended to emphasise the 'tough-on-crime' aspect of the government's message. So, too, was New Labour's acceptance of earlier Conservative reforms and proposals. This had started with the acceptance of the general approach of the 1994 Criminal Justice and Public Order Act and continued with New Labour's enactment, post-election, of mandatory minimum sentences for repeat offenders and with its borrowing of Michael Howard's proposals on parenting orders and curfews for development in its own legislation. It is not surprising, therefore, that the 1998 Act went through parliament with an unusual degree of cross-party agreement. The final set of youth justice measures in the Act constituted a programme that the Conservatives found difficult to oppose. These are summarised in Box 6.1:

Box 6.1   Crime and Disorder Act 1998: youth justice measures

New aim   'to prevent offending by children and young persons' (28:1) (applies to all agencies). This attempts to remove 'conflict between promoting the welfare of the child or young person and taking firm action to deal with his or her offending behaviour' (Home Office, 1998a, pp. 4–5).

YOTs   Each local authority to set up 'Youth Offending Teams' (involving police, probation, social services, education, health) to co-ordinate strategy.

Probation   Move away from care and towards 'risk assessment' and control.

Speed   Faster processing of offenders.

Age of criminal responsibility   Abolition of doli incapax.

Punishment   Greater use of secure accommodation and tagging for persistent offenders.

New orders
Reparation   This empowered courts to compel a young offender to make reparation to the victim of the offence or to society at large; perhaps through an apology and reparation to the victim (with the victim's consent) or through practical work in the local community.

Box 6.1   (Continued)

Anti-social behaviour   These 'can be applied for by the police or local authority, in consultation with each other, against an individual or several individuals (perhaps a family) whose behaviour is anti-social (for example, it causes alarm, distress or harassment to one or more people not in the same household as him/herself)' (Home Office, 1998b, p. 4).

Curfews   These apply to children under 10 (ages are specified in the order). They allow local authorities to impose a local curfew on unsupervised children between 9 p.m. and 6 a.m. (these were extended, in August 2002, to cover children up to the age of 15).

Child safety   These allow social services departments to use the Magistrates Court to ensure supervision of a child under 10 who is either at risk of anti-social behaviour or offending or has committed an act which would have been an offence had they been old enough, or has broken an already imposed, local child curfew.

Parenting   These orders attach to parents under certain conditions generated by the behaviour of their child. They can make the parent attend counselling or guidance sessions and/or impose requirements with respect to controlling the behaviour of their child (with respect to school attendance or avoiding certain people, for example).

Action plan   This empowers courts to impose a supervised 'action plan' on the offender for 3 months, setting out certain conditions with respect to their behaviour.

NB   The Act also contains a large number of changes to existing provisions (on Supervision Orders).

The specific relevance of each of these measures (for example, the various orders) to youth crime varies, but taken as a whole the Act is a major piece of legislation; possibly, in the words of one commentator in this field, 'the most radical overhaul of the youth justice system in fifty years' (Goldson, 2000, p. vi). Two of its key features merit further comment at this point, since they illustrate the main trends of government policy.

Youth Offending Teams (YOTs)

These are the key institutional innovation for dealing with youth crime at local level. The idea that locally based, multi-agency partnership arrangements were central to reducing crime was significantly influenced by the 1991 Morgan Report on 'safer communities' (Home Office, 1991) and had been supported by the Audit Commission (1996). The introduction of YOTs provides a central co-ordinating role for local authorities, who bring police, probation and the health service together to work with them in planning the provision of youth justice services and implementing a local youth justice plan. The inter-agency nature of these bodies is clear from their personnel. YOTs need to include at least one of the following: a social worker, a probation officer, a police officer, a person nominated by a local health authority in the area or a person nominated by the local authority's chief education officer. There is also scope to bring others – such as the voluntary sector – into this co-ordinating framework.

Co-ordination, oversight and standard-setting for YOTs is provided by a centrally appointed body, the Youth Justice Board for England and Wales (YJB). Because of this, the role of local authorities in YOTs does not necessarily mean more power and influence for them, since they are subject to strong auditing, oversight and quality control from the centre. For example, annual 'Youth Justice Plans' have to be submitted to the YJB for approval. The Board has a wide and powerful remit: advising the Home Secretary, overseeing the entire youth justice system, encouraging 'best practice', assessing performance, conducting research and awarding grants. Indeed, the establishment of the YJB and the commitment by both it and the government to fund research and to be guided by evidence on effectiveness are among the few things to be welcomed by some of those most critical of Labour's record in this area (Drakeford and Vanstone, 2000, p. 377; Hoyle and Rose, 2001, p. 77).

Abolition of doli incapax

This measure abolished the presumption that a child is incapable of telling the difference between right and wrong unless it can be shown otherwise – a presumption which had previously been applied to children aged between 10 and 13. Effectively, abolition means that any child over the age of 10 can now be treated in the same way with respect to deciding on whether to prosecute. One of Straw's arguments on this point was that the centuries-old rule of doli incapax had systematically allowed lawyers for defendants between the ages of 10 and 13 'to run rings round the court system, and to avoid proper sanctions for young offenders' (Hansard, 8 April 1998, col. 372). It was, however, an argument which ignored the fact that the UK's ages of criminal responsibility (Scotland's is eight) are much lower than those prevailing in most of the rest of Europe; Spain and Belgium, for example, have ages of 16 and 18 respectively (Coles and Maile, 2002, p. 289). It also ignored the recommendation of the United Nations Committee on the Rights of the Child that the UK should consider *raising* its age of criminal responsibility (United Nations Committee on the Rights of the Child, 1995).

The Youth Justice and Criminal Evidence Act 1999

A further piece of youth justice legislation was passed the following year, introducing a sentence of referral to a youth offender panel. Such panels consist of at least two volunteer lay members from the local community and a member of the local YOT. The measure applies to young offenders between the ages of 10 and 17 who plead guilty and are convicted for the first time by the courts. The rationale, as explained by Jack Straw in one of the relevant parliamentary debates, is that:

> all young offenders referred to youth offender panels will have to make reparation to their victims or to the wider community so that they understand the impact of their crimes. We are building on ideas of what has been described as restorative justice: a polysyllabic word designed to convey the idea that the justice system should try to restore some balance into the community and that the perpetrators of crime should deliver an element of justice to those who have been affected by them (Hansard, 15 April 1999, col. 385).

The model draws on the family conferencing approach in New Zealand and reparation experiments that had already been conducted by Thames Valley Police. The idea of reparation is not a new one and has been used before, though not through such an order. Referral orders seek to divert young offenders into a system with the aim of greater flexibility for working constructively and creatively with them, with a view to their reintegration into the community. Notwithstanding some reservations about insufficient levels of victim involvement and loss of discretion by magistrates, the final evaluation of the use of referral orders, based on the analysis of pilot projects, concluded that:

> All the major participants affected by the introduction of referral orders appear both to support the reforms in principle and to be broadly satisfied with the way in which they have been implemented in practice...In a short period of time referral orders have gone from being an interesting set of proposals to a generally robust set of working practices that, notwithstanding some of the tensions identified in this report, look set to have a considerable impact on the youth justice system in England and Wales (Newburn *et al.*, 2002, pp. 62–63).

On the strength of such confidence, the system of youth offender panels went 'live' nationally in April 2002. However, it does have its critics. As Muncie (2002) points out, although presented as a rehabilitative approach to young offenders under the age of 18 who plead guilty, the universal application of the referral order constitutes a significant threat to the use of conditional discharges for this group.

Children's rights and youth justice

Reference to children's rights is conspicuous by its absence in this area. Where the language of rights is used, it is generally in relation to a focus on the young person's welfare rather than their views and it is usually in the context of balancing their rights against those of victims. The Home Office applies this approach to the 'preventing offending' principle in the following manner:

> There must be consideration, by all agencies and individuals, of the welfare of the child or young person: this is required by the UN Convention on the Rights of the Child to which the UK is a signatory. But there must also be a balance between the interests of the child or young person who has offended and the interests of the victim, or potential victims (Home Office, 1998a, p. 5).

At first sight, it might seem that a more legalistic, authoritarian approach to youth justice is the most antithetical to children's rights. However, many have pointed out that 'welfare' approaches were by no means supportive of children's rights during the 1960s and 1970s. By drawing in potential offenders and minor offenders to the child welfare system, they often assumed a supervisory function for the state on sometimes dubious grounds.

Labour is using both approaches. On the one hand, ascribing to children as young as 10 adult responsibilities and sensibilities when crime occurs – or, in the words of Goldson, '"responsibilizing" children and "adultizing" childhood' (Goldson, 2001, p. 39) – can easily undermine any rights to welfare that they might previously be thought to have had. A number of key features of the new youth justice system can be highlighted in this regard, including the abolition of the doli incapax presumption. On the other hand, even in narrow 'justice model' terms, the imposition of restrictions on young people who may have committed no offence – through the use of child safety orders, local child curfews and anti-social behaviour orders – constitutes interference in the lives of young people that goes some way beyond a response to youth offending.

For this reason, such interventions may prove to be challengeable with respect to Article 6 (the right to a fair hearing) and Article 8 (respect for private and family life) of the European Convention on Human Rights. It is too early yet to say how much impact the 1998 Human Rights Act will have on youth justice processes. One straw in the wind is a change in procedures relating to offenders under the age of 18 who are found guilty of murder. Such offenders can now challenge, at reasonable intervals, the continued applicability of the sentence of being detained at Her Majesty's pleasure, on the grounds that the factors justifying such a sentence – the mental instability and dangerousness of the defendant – are susceptible to change over time. Other challenges upheld include those against the trial of children in adult courts in certain circumstances. More widely, a range of youth justice actions may prove to be challengeable on the grounds of their proportionality.

A further problem for New Labour's presentation of its approach comes from the United Nations. In October 2002, the United Nations Committee on the Rights of the Child (UNCRC) issued its second and most recent judgement on overall UK policy and practice with respect to children's rights (UNCRC, 2002). The 2002 report will have made uncomfortable reading for ministers and for a government that frequently presents itself as strongly committed to child welfare. Whilst acknowledging the Labour government's initiatives in areas such as child poverty, leaving care and participation in certain contexts, the report is highly critical of the UK government's approach and achievements with respect to the more specific subject of children's rights (Featherstone *et al.*, 2002).

The Committee's criticisms with respect to youth justice were on three main fronts: first, the retention of the age of criminal responsibility at 8 years in Scotland and 10 years in the rest of the UK; secondly, the increased use and length of custody for less serious offences; thirdly, the conditions in many young offender institutions. Given what we have noted already about the potential problems of the 1998 Crime and Disorder Act with respect to the UK's own human rights legislation, it is not surprising that the UNCRC believes that the Act 'may violate the principles and provisions of the Convention' (UNCRC, 2002: para. 57a). Its central concern, however, lies as much with the administration of justice as it does with the law itself.

> The Committee notes with serious concern that the situation of children in conflict with the law has worsened since the consideration of the initial report [1995] . . . children between 12 and 14 years of age are now being deprived of their liberty. More generally, the Committee is deeply concerned at the high and increasing numbers of children in custody; at earlier ages, for lesser offences and for longer custodial sentences imposed by the recent increased court powers to give detention and training orders . . . The Committee is also extremely concerned at the conditions that children experience in detention and that children do not receive adequate protection or help in young offender's institutions (for 15- to 17-year-olds), noting the very poor staff ratio, high levels of violence, bullying, self-harm and suicide (UNCRC, 2002, para. 57).

The list goes on. For good measure, the Committee also notes the figure of 296 children who sustained injuries following restraints and control in custody between April 2000 and February 2002 (UNCRC, 2002, para. 33).

Parents and parenting

With respect to parents, the implications of the 1998 Act are even clearer and the government is equally unapologetic in its justification of its basic approach.

It is neither possible nor desirable for the government to involve itself in every aspect of family life or to dictate to parents how to raise their children: parents hold the primary responsibility for giving children the love and care they need, ensuring their welfare and security and teaching them right from wrong. But the government can and should help parents to recognise and meet those responsibilities – and should strive to create the conditions in which families can flourish and all children have the chance to succeed (Home Office, 1997b, p. 9).

Notwithstanding Straw's careful wording, this is clearly a more interventionist approach to the family in the context of youth justice than had previously been the case under the Conservatives. Parenting, anti-social behaviour, child safety and curfew orders all have significant implications for parents. The linking of youth justice with interventionism on the parental front is not, of course, new. Even as far back as the 1963 Children and Young Persons Act, this was evident in the development of family advice centres in high-crime areas. What was new, however, was the compulsory, authoritarian flavour of the 1998 measures. Whilst there is some evidence that parenting support programmes more generally can reduce youth crime (see discussion below), it is the compulsory element of the current measures which has led many professionals to be dubious as to their potential efficacy (Henricson *et al.*, 2000). Furthermore, as we saw in Chapter 3, such programmes, despite the gender-neutral language, bear down disproportionately on poor women.

On the other hand, there is evidence of substantial public support for such an approach. The Home Office's own analysis of public attitudes to crime from the 1998 BCS showed 21 per cent of respondents identifying 'parental punishment and responsibility' as a sentencing option worth further use; way ahead of the next option (custodial sentences, at 13 per cent) (Mattinson and Mirrlees-Black, 2000, p. 24). It is therefore unsurprising that 'lack of discipline from parents' was identified as the main cause of crime by 28 per cent of respondents; once again, the highest figure (drugs came second, at 27 per cent) (Mattinson and Mirrlees-Black, 2000, p. 65).

The important question, of course, is whether parenting orders work. Research conducted on behalf of the Youth Justice Board investigated parenting programmes in which one-sixth of the participants had been referred through a Parenting Order while the rest had been referred voluntarily. Although the former were much more likely to feel negative about the programme at the outset, they were just as likely to feel positively about the schemes at the end as the voluntary majority. For both groups, 'exit' ratings were very positive, with only 6 per cent feeling negative or indifferent about the helpfulness of the programmes. The evaluation also noted that offending had been reduced by 50 per cent for the children of those attending parenting programmes, but was rightly cautious about attributing this to the programmes themselves (Ghate and Ramalla, 2002). On the strength of this assessment, Lord Warner, the then chair of the YJB, endorsed the continued use of such orders.

Targeting children

As already noted, New Labour's approach to this policy area incorporates a social policy analysis of the problem of youth crime. The New Labour mantra of being 'tough on crime, tough on the causes of crime'[2] implied a strong link to social policy of the kind that was frequently denied by Conservative crime spokespersons throughout the 1980s and 1990s. For example, the influential Audit Commission Report 'Misspent Youth' (1996, pp. 74–75, 80–82) recognised that young people either in or leaving the care system are an especially vulnerable group in the sense of exhibiting a number of risk factors associated with youth crime. Similarly, New Labour's post-election youth justice proposals cited a number of social policy measures as relevant to its youth crime agenda. These measures included its 'welfare to work' programme, the work of the Social Exclusion Unit, the Ministerial Group on the Family, the wider provision of nursery education and measures to tackle truancy and school exclusions (Home Office, 1997b, pp. 9–10).

A further reason for such an approach is that the factors linking youth crime to social structure also mean that members of Labour's own electoral constituency, or of social groups which it has traditionally sought to assist, are disproportionately affected as potential perpetrators, as well as victims, of crime. With respect to ethnicity in particular, even if evidence for the existence of major discrimination within the criminal justice system is partial (Smith, 1997) – and such a view has been challenged by some (Bowling and Phillips, 2002) – we do know that the system itself impacts disproportionately on certain groups such as black men of African-Caribbean origin. This alone should caution any social democratic party against using that system as its sole or overwhelming route for tackling crime. A twin-pronged approach of the kind that

Labour advocates is in part an attempt to minimise the possibility that it will merely be viewed as a punitive policy towards particular minorities.

With respect to those young people who do come within the youth justice net, the picture is somewhat different. Through its criminal justice measures, the Labour government has significantly enhanced the potential coercive powers of the local state with respect to young people (through the use of curfews, anti-social behaviour orders and child safety orders). For example, while Anti-Social Behaviour Orders (ASBOs) were intended for both adults and young people, being available for any offender aged 10 or over, they have most frequently been used on young people. Fifty-eight per cent of the ASBOs used between April 1999 and September 2001 were with respect to young people aged 18 or younger (Campbell, 2002, p. 8). YOTs and Youth Offender Panels are the instruments of this increased local interventionism. By its own measures, the government counts its interventionist strategy to be beneficial in a number of respects. For example, based on an analysis of some of the 466 ASBOs issued between April 1999 and September 2001, the Home Office research department claimed that, notwithstanding some bureaucratic and inter-agency problems:

> The overall opinion in the areas visited was generally positive. When used effectively, ASBOs have been successful in curbing unruly behaviour, have helped rebuild the quality of life in communities and cemented good relationships both between partner agencies and between these agencies and the community (Campbell, 2002, p. 6).

That said, while the slow initial take-up of ASBOs gradually increased in tempo, the widely varying levels of use of this measure were striking; some local areas made extensive use of them and others made little or no use (Reid, 2002, pp. 205–222).

It is clear that the increased interventionism of recent years that was evident with respect to looked after children is replicated in youth justice. Whilst this can be seen as its 'dark side' (Platt, 2000), New Labour's concern here is wider; with the victims of youth offending, many of whom are other young people (see Coles and Maile, 2002, pp. 300–310), as well as with offenders. Also, it claims that its approach is protective of the long-term interests of young offenders themselves. However, continuity with Conservative approaches rather than being a genuine 'Third Way' alternative means that it is no surprise that leading 'Third Way' advocate

Anthony Giddens was less than impressed with Labour's first-term record in this field, suggesting that 'Labour's policies continue to look disturbingly like those of the outgoing Tory government, with its defined streak of authoritarianism' (Giddens, 2002, p. 27).

Such an approach continued up to and beyond the 2001 General Election. Crime figures had fallen significantly and the numbers of young people found guilty or cautioned for offences fell between 1995 and 2000 (Coles and Maile, 2002, p. 292). Even though recorded crime had risen between 1998/1999 and 2001/2002, BCS data showed crime falling persistently, by 7 per cent overall, between 1997 and 2001 (having risen steadily under the Conservatives since 1981) (Simmons *et al.*, 2002, pp. 14, 16). However, public perceptions differed from reality and the government chose to accept public perceptions and continue with an authoritarian approach. At the 2001 election, 'law and order' was the third most important issue for voters and Labour was 2 per cent ahead of the Conservatives with respect to having the best policies on the issue – an improvement on 1997 (Worcester and Mortimore, 2001, p. 30). From virtually ignoring crime in its electoral appeals 20 years ago, Labour can be argued to be overemphasising it now. It did not help that it accepted so uncritically, and was influenced so heavily by, the analysis of the Audit Commission (1996, 1998). This analysis has been the subject of trenchant criticism (Jones, 2001), the most significant point of which is that it overemphasised both the extent of the problem of youth crime and the inadequacies of the then-prevailing system for dealing with it.

A number of measures quickly confirmed that the Home Secretary following the 2001 election, David Blunkett, was even more interventionist than Jack Straw (Home Office, 2001). First, the passage of the Anti-Social Behaviour Act in 2003, extending the powers of local authorities in this area. Secondly, there was an extension of the curfew option to children up to the age of 15 from August 2002; this was in spite of no local authority having yet used it for the lower age range.

Conclusion

It is difficult to know how to judge New Labour when it comes to the complexities of criminal behaviour. Judged solely in terms of crime statistics, they appear successful. A fall of 9 per cent in 2002, according to the BCS, and 7 per cent in recorded crime confirmed the trends already discussed (Home Office, 2003a). However, judgement on such a basis is always highly dubious, given the role of demographic, social, cultural and economic factors over which governments have little or no control. Charman and Savage's 'report card' approach to Labour's record (Charman and Savage, 2002, p. 221) allows us to note that they had fulfilled or were on the way to fulfilling their specific manifesto proposals on youth justice by the time of the 2001 General Election. For example, Labour's promise to half the time from arrest to sentence was achieved in mid-2002 and reconviction rates for young offenders have fallen by 22.5 per cent since 1997 (although the methodology for measuring this can be questioned; see Smith, 2002) – a measure the government attributes to the introduction of its reprimands and final warnings approach (Home Office, 2003a). However, Charman and Savage also note that the actual take-up of a number of Labour's initiatives has been slow; this particularly applies to child safety orders, child curfew orders and parenting orders. If such measures constitute a form of net-widening, as some critics have suggested, then this lack of take-up may be no bad thing.

The evaluation of other commentators on Labour's youth justice programme varies considerably. Both Hendrick (2003) and Smith (Smith, R., 2003) have been highly critical of recent developments; the former with particular emphasis on the effects of the increased use of custody on young offenders and the latter with respect to Labour's claims of success, questioning both the targets used and the methods of assessment. Others (Smith, D., 2003) take a more mixed view, noting the lower cautioning and conviction numbers between 1990 and 2000, the positive evaluations of parenting orders and referral orders and the reorganisation of the youth justice service to promote greater inter-agency working. All three critics, however, note the highly worrying trend towards the increased use of custodial sentences for young people. In January 1996, there were approximately 8500 young prisoners (15–20 years old). This had risen to 10,963 by December 2003 (Hollis and Goodman, 2003, p. 12). Moreover, increases at the lower age range have been particularly steep. For example, the juvenile population (15–17 years old) increased by 10 per cent between December 2001 and December 2002 (Hollis and Goodman, 2003, p. 14). That Labour intends to continue this basic approach is evident from its decision to publish a separate 'youth justice' companion to the 'Children at Risk' Green Paper (Home Office, 2003b) rather than incorporate its ideas within the Green Paper proper. Likewise, the content of the youth justice proposals promises an endorsement of the strategy of the

1998 Act alongside increased interventionism with parents and young people.

One feature of what is happening – and it stretches across other policy areas such as education – is the increasing social control of childhood.

> In spite of the UN Convention ... and all of the political rhetoric about children and their rights to be heard, it can be argued that this may, in effect, amount to little more than an artifice which conceals the real nature of the way in which mechanisms for retaining and increasing the control over children are being sustained and even extended. It would appear that the net of social control has an increasingly fine mesh and is permeating more areas of more children's lives than ever before (James and James, 2001, pp. 225–226).

That this applies with particular force in the field of youth justice is evident from all that has been said, but it is not only applicable to this field. Authoritarian measures are now being applied outside of the normal parameters of the youth justice system – in working with parents and with disaffected young people – and with implications for workers in those environments. Secondly, there is a trend towards the use of custody for more and younger children. Thirdly, there is a general assumption by the New Labour government that authoritarian means can be justifiably and effectively used for desirable ends and that unintended consequences will be few. This is an optimistic prospectus in this context, given what we know about the generally poor impact of custody on reoffending rates and the potential for labelling through the net-widening measures of the Crime and Disorder Act. It is possible that Labour's approach, imaginative as it is in some respects, will eventually undermine its early achievements by overuse of a punitive strategy that stores up long-term reoffending.

Notes

1. The 2001 general election manifesto offered an endorsement and continuation of the above strategy, together with a little more on the 'tackling the causes of crime' front: improved custodial accommodation and programmes for 18–20-year-old offenders, school drugs education and youth inclusion schemes for high-crime areas (Labour Party, 2001, pp. 31–32).
2. Ironically, one of the phrases for which Blair will be best remembered was provided by Gordon Brown (Rentoul, 2001, p. 193).

CHAPTER 7

Disabled Children and Young People

Introduction

In studies of the history of disability, there is evidence of disabled children being perceived in various ways. These include perceptions of such children as expendable, as a defective and weakening social element and as personifications of evil. On the other hand, this diverse grouping of children and young people has also been seen as gifts from God and, as such, in need of compassion and protection (Oswin, 1984). In the UK, disabled children have to compete for resources in a society where fast-developing research in the field of genetics tempts prospective parents with visions of a perfect or 'designer' child and where the abortion of a damaged foetus is regarded by large numbers of people as a responsible and justifiable course of action.

For most writers and activists in this field, terminology is particularly important in relation to disability. Referring to an individual with impairments as a disabled person has been seen by proponents of social models of disability as a way of drawing attention to the external constraints which 'disable'. The Children Act (1989) uses the phrase 'children with disabilities' and by doing so attempts to make it clear that children with disabilities are children first. This chapter will refer to *disabled children and young people* in order to reflect the barriers that are experienced by such children and young people. However, it also seeks to emphasise in its analysis that disabled children are primarily children first and share the same range of ambitions, hopes and fears as other children (Middleton, 1999).

There is a considerable historical legacy of treating disabled children differently. This became entrenched in policy and practice frameworks in the UK from the mid-nineteenth century onwards. During the nineteenth century and much of the twentieth century, many disabled children spent their lives in long-stay institutions and it is pertinent to note that this form of provision went into decline only in the 1970s. Indeed, long-stay institutions were used to provide short-term care up until the late 1980s; a practice which Oswin (1984) maintained could only be described as 'kennelling'. Middleton (1999) notes that respite care, that is, non-home-based residential provision, still remains the main plank of welfare provision for disabled children and their parents. She emphasises that it continues to be used in circumstances which would be viewed as unacceptable for non-disabled children of the same age.

It is also important to note that disabled children are much more likely to be looked after. A re-analysis of Office of Population Census Surveys (OPCS) material undertaken by Ball (1998) found that at the time of the surveys 5.7 per cent of disabled children, compared to 0.6 per cent of non-disabled children, were being looked after by local authorities. These children were predominantly placed in residential and foster care establishments, with some at boarding schools. Additionally, Abbott *et al.* (2000) have pointed out that many children regarded as living at home are actually placed at special residential schools for the duration of the school term. Morris (1997), in an evocatively titled article, 'Gone Missing', which reports on her research into children living away from home, highlights the effects of segregation and separation and the impact of sustained contact with disabling and at times abusive systems on children.

A dominant understanding is that children experience continuous change in relation to their physical abilities, their levels of understanding and their emotions and that these in turn are influenced by environmental factors, by social and cultural practices and by gendered expectations. Most children are expected to grow to a position of increased autonomy, to interact with their broadening environment and to expand their opportunities. Opportunities can be limited by the interactive operation of social divisions such as class and gender, but constraints are not necessarily immutable. For disabled children, such a dynamic view of childhood is less readily accepted. Phrases such as 'he's got the IQ of a three-year-old' or 'she's a baby really' can be seen to retain an enduring dominance. Moreover, children with physical impairments are often assumed to have learning impairments also.

Children with physical and intellectual impairments can face increasing restrictions and constricting horizons as they get older. Developmental impairments rather than abilities can be accentuated and considerations of safety, both in relation to physical safety and protection from exploitation, can easily deny disabled young people the opportunity to learn from varied experiences. Emphasis can be placed on independence – defined, for example, as the ability to get dressed without personal assistance – rather than on autonomy; defined in terms of making decisions, taking personal responsibility and making choices. Social models of disability, as developed by Oliver (1983, 1990), Oliver and Barnes (1998), Barnes and Mercer (1996), Morris (1993, 1996), Hales (1996), Barton and Oliver (1997), Drake (1999), Corker and French (1999) and Barnes *et al.* (1999), challenge these disabling scenarios.

However, it is also the case that understandings of disability have changed significantly over the past 20 years. Disability rights movements, which have placed emphasis on social models of disability, have stressed that disabled people are not disadvantaged by impairments but by segregationalist and objectifying social, cultural, political and economic practices. Categorisations of impairments have been rejected in favour of specific measures to tackle disablism. The Disability Discrimination Act (1995), although still limited in its provisions and retaining a medicalised orientation, makes it illegal to discriminate against a disabled person with regard to employment, goods, facilities and services. Whilst there are exclusions, this Act is notable in that for the first time in the UK discrimination against disabled people in specified areas is subject to legal prohibitions. The Act also requires schools to comment in their annual reports on their arrangements for the admission of disabled pupils, the steps that they have taken to prevent disabled pupils being treated less favourably and upon facilities for disabled access. The significance of the Act for disabled children and young people is that, whilst it requires further development, it sets benchmarks with regard to legally sanctioned acceptable and unacceptable practices. It also paves the way for further legislation, such as that incorporated in the draft Disability Discrimination Bill (2004).

A number of policies and practices which have been initiated by New Labour, and those which continue to be supported by them, clearly contain positive and developmental aspects. However, these can also be seen to be intertwined with significant contradictions and constraints. Both the positive developments and the constraints will be considered in this chapter in the course of an examination of how policies that are associated with the development of a social investment state have impacted upon disabled children and young people. In considering disabled children in relation to New Labour's emphasis on the social investment state, one notices three key tensions: with respect to social inclusion and citizenship, there is a tension between work and care; with respect to investing through parents, there is a tension between surveillance and support; and finally, with respect to investing in children there is a tension between targeting and rights.

Social inclusion and citizenship: work vs 'care'

New Labour came to power in 1997 on a wave of popular enthusiasm which contained high expectations that policies and practices with regard to marginalised groupings of people would change radically. However, the high expectations of the disability lobby were quickly dashed when the New Labour administration continued to implement Conservative benefit cuts and restrict eligibility to benefits. Instead of introducing policies and practices to tackle the structural inequalities faced by disabled people, New Labour focused upon promoting social inclusion and on preventing social exclusion by both redefining and re-emphasising the concept of citizenship. As part of this process, the traditional structural analyses of disadvantage of 'Old' Labour and concerns about the creation of a level playing field gave way to a focus on the individual as shaped by personal circumstances and on the redefinition of rights and obligations between the individual and the community (Giddens, 1998). This approach has resulted in obligations being linked to rights and to citizenship becoming an implicit contract between the individual and the state. Accordingly, if obligations and responsibilities, which are primarily linked to work, are fulfilled, then individuals become entitled to legislatively specific rights. Those unable to meet such obligations and responsibilities, perhaps aptly, if superficially, summed up in the slogan 'work for those who can, security for those who can't', are entitled to 'care', which continues to carry with it both a protective and a controlling element.

Disabled children and young people, like all children and young people in the UK, are finding that they have to learn how to be good citizens and to earn the right to citizenship by striving to enter the labour market. However, research published by The Joseph Rowntree Foundation shows that disabled young people who are regarded as being capable of work have to continue to contend with entrenched segregationalist mechanisms. For example, it has been shown that as part of New Deal arrangements, disabled young people are more likely to be assigned to short-term, minimum-wage environmental task forces which usually result in long-term employment marginalisation rather than in real earning potential (Craig, 2001; Britton *et al.*, 2002).

Alongside such labour market difficulties, inherent contradictions also persist in the benefit system and these continue to adversely affect disabled young people of working age. Under the 'All Work Test', those disabled claimants who are tested and found to be eligible for incapacity and/or disability benefits administered by the Department of Work and Pensions have to continue to emphasise inability and incapacity in order to continue to receive targeted payments. Jordan and Jordan (2000) have argued that a system which separates claimants into those who have been deemed ineligible for benefit, those who are eligible for Disability Credit but are required to work, and those who are eligible for incapacity and/or disability benefits, does not promote social inclusion and integration:

> Their (Labour Government) narrow conceptions of work and independence preclude consideration of many of the aspects most significant for people with disabilities. Welfare service users face a battery of assessments, paternalistic packages of help and compulsory 'inclusions', and strong pressures to comply with these categorizations (Jordan and Jordan, 2000, p. 123).

The paradox between the promoted goal of social inclusion and the exclusionary mechanisms of the benefit process can leave young disabled people stranded between positive rhetoric and the dispiriting reality of the current work/benefits system.

For those who are unable to work, there are further difficulties. Despite changes to political and theoretical understandings, the position of those perceived as 'vulnerable' and promised or deemed to require 'security', is far from straightforward. Key documents such as Modernising Social Services (DoH, 1998a) accentuate the importance of making the system 'more centred on service users' (p. 13, 2.4) and advocate independence rather than dependency. However, the emphasis placed in this document on improving protection, albeit in the context of improving the regulatory framework for agencies, far outweighs exhortations to meaningfully involve service users in the design of their own care packages and in service provision more generally. As a result, caring responsibilities, be they formal or informal, continue to carry the implicit message that key decisions and boundary setting as to what the 'care' entails are the prerogative of the carer or the caring agency.

Investing through parents: support vs surveillance

The New Labour agenda places emphasis on regarding the family, which includes the 'corporate family', as an 'energising unit which can strengthen the ability of children to become citizens' (Platt, 2000, p. 5). Parents appear as the key element in ensuring the welfare of disabled children and young people, with clear mechanisms also being put in place to promote the achievements and well-being of looked after children. However, within this emphasis on parents, there are tensions that stem from the promotion of a dual focus on both support and also on surveillance or control. Moreover, the nature of the support on offer from the state can be seen to differ substantially from what research reports in this field say about what parents themselves say they want.

An example of this tension between support and surveillance can be found in the Framework for the Assessment of Children in Need and their Families (Department of Health, 2000a). As well as being closely linked to the QP initiative, this framework forms an important part of the government's social inclusion agenda for disabled children and young people. However, the policy and practice developments stemming from the framework are based on the Children Act 1989 and in relation to disabled children the implications of this Act have always been mixed. On the one hand, the 1989 Act provides a cohesive legal framework for all children and, by including disabled children within it, emphasises the inclusionary principle that such children are 'children first'. On the other hand, this inclusionary feature is diluted by the retention of medicalised definitions of disability and by the insistence that *all* disabled children, by virtue of their impairments, are 'children in need'. Moreover, although all social services departments have responsibility for disabled children, there has been marked disagreement about definitions of disability in relation to particular services and about which agency has primary responsibility for providing such services.

The Framework was intended to be holistic, with an integrated assessment process that examines all aspects of a child's life in relation to the child's developmental needs, the parent/child relationship and the prevailing social environment. The introductory section of the Practice Guidance, which focuses upon disabled children (Department of Health, 2000b), emphasises the importance of overcoming disabling barriers and incorporating understandings derived from the social model of disability into working practices. However, those sections which stipulate the details of the assessment process adopt a different tone. A request for support within the context of the framework can trigger a multi-disciplinary assessment which looks at: the children's developmental needs, their health, their education, their emotional and behavioural development, their family and social relationships, their social presentation; their self-care skills, their safety and the levels of stimulation they are offered. Such a wide-ranging assessment could be viewed by a parent of a disabled child as exhaustive and overly intrusive rather than as holistic. Additionally, the attention paid in the Framework documentation to questionnaires and rating scales, administered and analysed by a third party, can further distance parents, carers, disabled children and young people from their assessment of their situation.

There are clear problem areas to be addressed, in that in practice settings disabled children and their families are subject to a number of uncoordinated assessments by a variety of different agencies. It also has to be acknowledged that the resources that are required to provide realistic support to families have additionally not been forthcoming. Some parents have undoubtedly found the Assessment Framework helpful in that it has added to the levels of professional support and resources available. A Department of Health evaluation of the impact of the Assessment Framework found that 75 per cent of parents interviewed reported that they felt they had been consulted and involved in all stages of the referral, assessment and planning process (Department of Health, 2003b). Nevertheless, the recorded levels of satisfaction with the resulting plans were far more mixed. This evaluation also provided messages for successful implementation. These highlighted the need for more training and for greater inter-agency collaboration at all levels.

However, the contradictory elements contained in the assessment process have the potential to exclude as well as include. The potential to exclude is highlighted by the ambiguity surrounding the extent to which parents are involved in the assessment process as it applies to parenting skills. The Assessment of Children in Need and their Families Practice Guidance states that:

> Parents should be clearly informed that their views and priorities are important and that they should be encouraged to contribute to the process. The process should include recognition of the parent/carer needs in bringing up their children (3.17, Department of Health, 2000b Practice Guidance).

In relation to the involvement of parents in the assessment process, a variety of approaches have been promoted. At one end of a hypothetical continuum, there is the view that professionals should work in full partnership with parents (Beresford, B., 1994). At the other end is the perspective that parents should be subject to professional assessments (Department of Health, 2000b, p. 95). The difference between these two positions reflects the capacity of professionals to work *with* parents and their capacity for carrying out assessments *on* parents. In practice, the distinction is rather more subtle, but this continuum raises important process issues and points to a very real divide between rhetoric and practice.

Research has pointed to the importance of service providers actively resourcing and supporting 'what works' for different parents (Beresford, 1994; Beresford, B., *et al.*, 1996; Russell, 1996; Read and Clements, 2001). Such research emphasises the importance of professionals fully acknowledging different styles and strategies, bearing in mind that information and discussion with informed others about a full range of options may improve the strategies adopted. It also highlights the absence of a blueprint for effective services and advocates the promotion of a user-centred, flexible, enabling and inclusive approach which recognises and responds to 'the complexities of unequal power relations' (Read and Clements, 2001, p. 19). In contrast, there is a danger that the interventionist approaches favoured by New Labour will not prove to be sufficiently flexible to be either helpful or supportive to parents. A government initiative called 'Together from the Start' (Department for Education and Skills, 2003) helps to illustrate this point. The aims of this initiative are to bring about effective early intervention, to promote partnership working between parents and professionals from the statutory and voluntary sectors, and to improve services overall for disabled children under three and their parents. However, this service, in terms of its utility for parents, can stand or fall in relation to interpretations of 'intervention'. The Association of Directors of

Social Services (ADSS) spokesperson for services for disabled children made this point forcibly when he said that such services for young disabled children and their families would be greatly improved if they started from the perspective of the rights of the child as services that give the child and their parents a voice are much more successful in meeting their needs (Matt Burkowski, in 'Time for an Early Start' [A.Unity Sale] CC 12–18 June 2003, pp. 32–33).

A further problem is that whilst investing through parents is a key plank of current government policy, it is also clearly one which can obscure children's own views and the roles that they play in each other's lives. In relation to the assessment process contained in the Framework for the Assessment of Children in Need and their Families (DoH, 2000a), there are further examples of ambiguities and contradictions. On the one hand, the documentation does point to the need for both separate and joint assessments with regard to disabled children and their parents. In relation to disabled children, the terms 'active involvement' and 'contribution' are used and it is acknowledged that recognition needs to be paid to 'their rights to be involved and consulted about matters which affect their lives' (DoH, 2000a, 3.41; DoH, 2000b, 3.15; DoH, 2000c, p. 10). On the other hand, as with adult services, different interpretations of what constitutes 'active involvement' have resulted in a wide variety of outcomes (Winchester, 2000). In this context, it is so notable that a recent survey carried out by the Disability Rights Commission (2002) found that 74 per cent of the young people surveyed believed that the government had limited awareness of their needs and rarely listened to what they had to say. Similarly, Shakespeare (2002), in a major study, highlights how the voices of parents, professionals and other adults continue to be prioritised over those of disabled children and young people, with damaging results.

As part of the large-scale research project 'Life as a Disabled Child', funded by the ESRC, Shakespeare involved more than 300 disabled children with a wide range of physical, cognitive and sensory impairments living in two locations in England and Scotland. The aims of the project were to explore perspectives of disability, the roles that children and young people adopted in negotiating their daily lives and the relationships, environments and structures which shaped their experiences. A key finding of the study was that disabled children were subject to a very high degree of surveillance by adults. Such children were found to have few social contacts outside the family and activities were often dominated by adult presence. Adults also mediated in terms of contact with other children, often serving to compound segregationalist practices, adversely influencing the attitudes of non-disabled children. Whilst disabled children identified with disability in many different ways, adults tended to emphasise the different and special needs of disabled children and to limit their range of responses.

Investing in children: targeting vs rights

New Labour have not targeted disabled children and young people for intervention to the same extent that other groups can be seen to have been targeted. One reason for this could be that disabled children do not fit into the social investment state as either 'threats' to civil order or 'opportunities' for promoting a more market-friendly society. This is not to say that disabled children have not been incorporated within the social inclusion agenda. This has happened in a variety of ways. In October 2000, for example, the QP programme was extended from 3 to 5 years, the money available was increased and £60m was specifically designated for improving services for disabled children. Additionally, £220m has been earmarked for improving the accessibility of mainstream schools for disabled children as part of the Special Educational Needs and Disability Act (2001). The Valuing People White Paper (Department of Health, 2001d) focused on tackling social exclusion and bringing about integration by focusing on all aspects of life for individuals with learning impairments. It stressed the importance of disabled children and young people maximising life opportunities by exerting control and choice, by leading positive lives and by fully participating in communities. The Carers and Disabled Children Act (2001), by means of direct payments, places emphasis on flexible and individualised support packages. The Special Educational Needs and Disability Act (2001) and the SEN Action Programme (Department for Education and Skills, 2003), in turn, are concerned to promote social inclusion by giving disabled students rights within the mainstream educational system and by tackling low attainment levels. These areas are reinforced by the Green Paper 'Every Child Matters' (2003). Additionally, in 2001, the National Information Centre for families of disabled children was established to provide more information about supportive services. Also, the Children and Young People's Unit has actively explored the needs and views of disabled children and young people by running a variety of workshops and focus groups (Dobson, 2001).

Moreover, disabled children and young people have been included in initiatives which relate to all children. These include projects such as Sure Start, Connexions and the Children's Fund. These aim to empower children to realise their full potential by utilising available opportunities. Similarly, the Department of Health Action Plan 'Listening, Hearing and Responding: Core Principles for the Involvement of Children' (Department of Health, 2001e) exhorts professionals to listen to children and to help them to attain their aspirations.

Although in a more limited way than elsewhere, with a more pronounced rhetorical rather than practical tone, the government can be seen to have prioritised a form of targeting, associated with social inclusion initiatives, over rights. Whilst this form of targeting can be used as a means of narrowing the divide between disabled and non-disabled children, it can also further accentuate segregation rather than inclusion on the basis of specific requirements or 'special needs'. An appraisal of the historical and contemporary debates about the education of disabled children and young people serves to illustrate these points.

Education has an extremely important place in the New Labour project. In addition to the development of academic and vocational abilities, education influences socialisation processes and how children view themselves and are viewed by others. It is therefore regarded by politicians and policy-makers as a way of preparing children for adulthood and responsible citizenship. Until relatively recently, disabled children were prevented from entering the mainstream education system. Initially, this was through the exclusion of those disabled children defined as 'ineducable' by the 1944 Education Act and subsequently by the segregated 'special' school system.

From the passing of the 1944 Education Act up until the introduction of the 1970 Education Act, disabled children were able to access educational opportunities only if they were classified as being able to benefit from these. As a result, large numbers of disabled children were deemed to be 'ineducable'. The 1981 Education Act, drawing upon the Warnock Report (1978), focused upon providing an inclusive education for disabled children and introduced the 'statementing' procedure which obliged local educational authorities ('where necessary') to detail and meet special educational requirements. It also changed the terminology used, with various forms of 'handicap' being redesignated as 'special educational need'. The term 'learning difficulty' was also brought in to replace the label 'educationally subnormal'. The 1981 Act has been revised and updated and the current legislative framework is now informed by the far more progressive 1996 Education Act. However, the complexity of the procedure for accessing mainstream education, the time taken to produce and act upon detailed statements of need and a continued emphasis on identifying and meeting 'special' need remain constraining and excluding factors for disabled children.

Prior to the introduction of measures to support disabled children attending mainstream schools, the main form of educational provision available focused on disabled children attending specialist schools, many on a residential basis. The practice of placing disabled children and young people in special schools has been severely criticised by organisations of disabled people such as 'People First' and by writers from within the disability lobby (for example, Barnes *et al.*, 1999). They stress the importance of disabled children being integrated within the mainstream system, arguing that segregated schools concentrate on impairments, disabilities, the development of coping mechanisms for restricted environments and approximations of 'normality' rather than on the skills required for tackling disabling practices. However, it is important to acknowledge that organisations of those with hearing and visual impairments, in particular, contest assertions that specialist schooling is limited and constraining and maintain that specialist provision better equips children and young people to maximise their potential in adult life.

It is clear that a policy which emphasises targeting contains the seeds of exclusion rather than inclusion. Moreover, a legislative development such as the Special Educational Needs and Disability Act (2001), as illustrated by its title, continues to utilise the language of exclusion rather than inclusion and to contain exclusionary as well as inclusionary practices. Recent research carried out by Jenny Morris (2001) in association with SCOPE draws attention to the fact that although there have been some improvements which are to be welcomed relating to education, direct payments for personal assistance and legislative measures to address active discrimination, basic issues are still not being addressed for disabled young people with high support needs. Morris used a variety of techniques to explore with young people what they felt about the quality of their lives and what they understood by social exclusion. Forty-four young people with complex needs, between the ages of 15 and 20, participated in the study. Young people regarded as having communication difficulties were found to be excluded from participating in discussions about their needs, decision-making processes and those activities available to other young people. Overall, current services were seen to have major failings. In addition to agencies not addressing the need for assistance with communication, other exclusionary practices included the following: not being listened to, a lack of control over decisions about what happens to you, feeling unsafe and limited opportunity to be included in local community activities. As Dobson (2001) points out, the Scope Report (2001) suggests that policy-makers need to focus social exclusion measures on policies that can deliver basic human rights as well as on employment, education and community participation.

One possible way of developing more inclusionary policies is to target shortfalls in the attainability of goals, rather than targeting disabled children and young people themselves; with the goals for all children being the same. This builds on the arguments utilised by the Disability Rights Movement. This means that agreed goals would be used as a yardstick to measure discrepancies. This approach links targeting to rights in the sense that disabled children, like all children, have the right to aim for and to be supported to obtain the same goals as other children. However, this raises the question of the extent to which current shortfalls have been addressed. A useful area to focus on here is the success or failure of integrationalist policies in mainstream schools.

The extent to which educational provision within mainstream schools promotes integration rather than segregation has been subject to much debate. Discussions have focused on 'supported' and 'specialised' mainstream school placements. According to Barnes *et al.* (1999), the former contains the language of inclusion, whilst the latter retains the terminology of segregation. Priestley (1999) has analysed information collected as part of the ESRC-funded 'Life as a Disabled Child' project referred to earlier. He focuses on the experiences and perceptions of 20 disabled children and young people in the 6–16 age range. His analysis supports Shakespeare's arguments (2002) and highlights the ways in which disabled children can become differentially constructed within a mainstream school by means of formal and informal practices.

Priestley found that disabled children taking the same classes as their non-disabled peers were isolated from others in their class as a result of the provision of specialist support staff. The formalisation of helping relationships between disabled and non-disabled children by teachers also had the potential to infringe upon and alter the nature of the relationship between the children. This sometimes resulted in the helper being required to 'speak for' and intervene 'on behalf of' the disabled child, creating a relational power imbalance. Priestley (1999) noted that teachers tended to treat homework produced by disabled children as more of a bonus than a requirement and promoted the social rather than the academic benefits of mainstream schooling. Disabled children were also not subject to the same disciplinary processes as non-disabled children – a fact which did not go unnoticed by non-disabled children, causing them to emphasise difference rather than acknowledge sameness.

As part of this project, the ways in which disabled children and young people responded to these differential constructions and how they developed and retained feelings of self-esteem and self-worth were also explored. Priestley (1999) found that disabled children and young people clearly rejected negative disability labels from other students, using a variety of strategies and techniques, but that they skilfully manipulated disabled identities when they thought it could work to their advantage. Priestley comments that disability discourses within schools can place pressure on disabled children to identify with one of two logically opposing and hierarchically arranged categories – disabled or non-disabled. He found that the identifications chosen can affect peer group preferences, although considerations of age and gender could intervene and prove stronger than disabled or non-disabled identifications.

Priestley contends that while the integration of children with impairments into mainstream schools has provided many opportunities and has served to blur the boundaries between 'disabled' and 'non-disabled', especially amongst children themselves, the language of 'special need' and the associated practices which operate at both formal and informal levels can counter such blurring and can continue to segregate disabled children. Accordingly, the continued operation of often unintentional exclusionary practices within school systems needs to be tackled before inclusion and integration can become a reality for disabled children and young people.

In summary, there are gaps and inconsistencies in the New Labour project in relation to disabled children. It is clear that although some progress is being made in relation to targeting the attainability of goals (for example, by means of some of the provisions contained in The Special Educational Needs and Disability Act (2001), The Carers and Disabled Children Act (2001) and developments such as the National Information Centre for families of disabled children and the Children and Young People's Unit), exclusionary mechanisms continue to operate. There is also a basic tension between rhetoric and practice, with varying interpretations operating at national and local levels with regard to the operation of legislation and the carrying out of initiatives.

Conclusion

New Labour has been prescriptive about the shape public services for disabled children are to take and has supported this with some resources. However, their prescription for and emphasis on intervention contains both the strengths and the weaknesses of their approach. The Framework for the Assessment of Children in Need and their Families (DoH, 2000a) is a good example. It is well intentioned, but its scrutinising and controlling aspects have the potential to deter rather than to encourage. Aldridge and Becker (1994), amongst others, have drawn attention in their research findings to families choosing not to seek professional help because they fear losing control of events. Over-intrusive assessment processes could clearly cause parents of disabled children not to seek support, thus exacerbating social exclusion.

The emphasis placed by New Labour on parents as a means of ensuring the welfare of children is also potentially constraining for disabled children and young people. Despite policy documents highlighting the importance of hearing the voices of disabled children, insufficient attention continues to be paid to the ways in which others mediate for them. It remains rare for disabled children to be considered outside of the context of parent/child relationships and, as noted, parents and adults can both intentionally and unintentionally restrict contact with peers and limit social and educational opportunities.

An emphasis on targeting as opposed to promoting children's rights also contains exclusionary mechanisms. With regard to disabled children and young people, a more pronounced focus on rights is imperative if individual young people are to achieve their potential. This would involve a change of orientation of the current administration from a concentration on targeting and intervention to a practical rather than a rhetorical focus on choice, flexibility and collaboration.

In conclusion, current policy agendas for disabled children and young people can be seen to contain developmental aspects as well as contradictions and constraints. The work vs 'care' tension demonstrates how investment in inclusionary initiatives centred around work bring with them exclusionary divisions which can perpetuate care and control practices. Policies and procedures which continue to place emphasis on support and surveillance continue to give parents what the government think they need rather than what they say they want and to obscure the voices of disabled children.

In turn, a focus on targeting vs rights can fail to deliver basic human rights to those perceived as vulnerable.

The policy and practice framework promoted by New Labour has the potential to improve the opportunities available for disabled children and young people. However, whilst the rhetoric at the heart of recent developments emphasises active participation by children and young people, political concerns about control over policy and practice point to the continuation of a system with authority over outcomes remaining in the hands of centralised bodies. Proponents of the social model of disability have campaigned for the rights, citizenship and full integration of disabled people into society. As argued earlier, this has led to a radical reappraisal of understandings of disability and to gains for those regarded as responsible and capable of participating in the workforce. However, the picture for those viewed as vulnerable and in need of security, at both policy and practice levels, is more complex. Change is not just about setting targets for the commissioners and providers of services, but about focusing on civil rights issues and the barriers to full integration. These are not static processes, but areas which need to be continually interrogated and addressed.

CHAPTER 8

Children, Young People and Mental Health

Introduction

More and more children are experiencing mental ill health according to a range of statistics (Meltzer *et al.*, 2000). Social Trends (2002), for example, reports that one in 10 children under the age of 11 has been diagnosed as suffering from a mental health condition. The World Health Organisation and the United Nations Children's Fund have stated that up to one in five of the world's children are suffering from mental health or behavioural problems (BBC News, 2002). The reasons for this are far from clear cut. Undoubtedly, the pressures which children and young people now have to face are considerable, with image, achievement (or non-achievement), parental poverty and peer group pressure featuring significantly. The various ways in which differences relating to class, gender, disability, sexuality and ethnicity intersect and impact on some children and young people will also make a difference (Coleman and Schofield, 2001). However, incidence statistics alone only give a partial picture and the various ways in which mental health problems can be socially constructed also requires interrogation.

New Labour began to significantly focus on the mental health needs of children and young people after the 2000 General Election, when CAMHS incorporated into the planned National Service Framework for Children. Also, the Green Paper 'Every Child Matters' (2003) recommended a 10 per cent increase in CAMHS capacity each year for the following 3 years and for all areas to have in place comprehensive CAMHS by 2006. However, mental health services for children and young people continue to be described as under-resourced, inadequately staffed, fragmented and ill-equipped to deal with the needs of children and young people (The Mental

Health Foundation, 2001; Kurtz, 2003). Although more government money is being allocated, the direction that services should take is far from straightforward. This chapter begins by examining the background to the current situation concerning children and young people by looking at debates and policy initiatives in the field of adult mental health services. Mental health, the diagnosis of mental ill health and the meeting of needs are not clear-cut issues and there is much debate about constructions, definitions, practices and ways forward. Discussions about adult mental health services have considerable relevance for children and young people and the ways in which New Labour has responded to key issues are appraised in this chapter. These issues include the continued location of mental health problems within a medicalised framework, the implications for children and young people of a National Service Framework, and issues of rights and the potential for conflict between children, young people and their families. The chapter concludes by considering the ways in which New Labour has invested in mental health services for children and young people.

Adult mental health services: debates and policies

The arena of 'mental health' has long been beset by different ways of conceptualising and responding to what has variously been termed mental distress, mental ill health, mental illness and madness. There are conceptualisations which locate mental health firmly within medicalised parameters. Here, mental health difficulties are viewed as illnesses with symptoms which can be categorised and treated predominantly, but not exclusively, with drug and physical treatments (for example, Linford Rees, 1978; Howe, 1995). Social factors are taken into account, particularly in terms of assessing risk, but medication predominates with regard to treatment. These approaches have been contrasted with more socially-oriented models which focus on removing stigma, stressing citizenship rights and promoting a broader-based response to 'mental distress' (for example, Prior, 1993; Pilgrim and Rogers, 1996, 1999; Sayce, 2000; Beresford, 2001). The very terminology used can be seen to highlight different allegiances. The use of terms relating to mental ill health or illness, for example, firmly centre discussions within medicalised frames of reference. Terms such as 'mental distress' broaden the conceptual range, placing difficulties experienced on a continuum where it is acknowledged that we all experience problems at various points in time with some being more severe than others. There is also the use of the originally pejorative term 'madness' reused and revalued as a positive statement of difference, to consider. Commentators such as Rachel Perkins (1999) present the view that minimising difference via the apparently inclusive language of distress is unhelpful and illusory. Passing as 'sane' and denying difference is seen to perpetuate oppression. Perkins (1999), drawing from black and lesbian/gay politics, insists that real inclusion can be achieved only by the celebration of difference and diversity. She suggests: 'so let's dispense with notions of distress and embrace mad pride' (Perkins, 1999, p. 6). However, despite varying interpretations and differing terminologies, it would be unhelpful to suggest that the perspectives (although sometimes presented as such) are mutually exclusive. There is considerable overlap. Although it is important to highlight that medicalised perspectives retain dominance in relation to resources, services and policy, these are increasingly informed and influenced by more socially-oriented approaches.

In the UK, policy is changing rapidly in the field of 'mental health'. New Labour has produced key policy documents which include the White Paper 'Modernising Mental Health Services' (DoH, 1998b), the National Service Framework for Mental Health (2000) and a proposed reform of the 1983 Mental Health Act which changes the ways in which people broadly diagnosed as suffering from a 'mental disorder' can be compulsorily detained and/or treated.

In the White Paper 'Modernising Mental Health Services' (DoH, 1998b), areas which have been prioritised include the improved assessment of individual needs, better treatment and care both at home and in hospital, and access to services on a 24-hour basis. Emphasis has been placed on ensuring public safety and managing risk and upon mental health services being based in primary care settings with close links being maintained with specialist teams to integrate service planning and delivery. Close partnerships with education, employment and housing departments have been promoted and the need for patients, service users and carers to be involved, both in their own care and in planning services, has been highlighted within this frame of reference. Cost-effectiveness and 'Best Value' have remained central to service provision, with the National Institute for Clinical Excellence providing guidance.

The National Service Framework for Mental Health (2000) has emphasised the importance of strengthening partnerships between the National Health Service and social care organisations. The Framework incorporates standards relating to five main areas. These are: mental health promotion, primary care and access to services, services for people with severe mental illness, support for carers, and the prevention of suicide. The standards are linked to existing statistics and milestones, and performance indicators have been specified in order to measure progress.

The much-delayed reform of the Mental Health Act 1983 looks to modernise services by authorising compulsory treatment in the community as part of an agreed care plan. This remains controversial and has been taken to demonstrate the prioritisation of drug therapies and the protection of the public over service user choice and social inclusion as citizens. The proposed reforms also remove the independent non-clinical role of the Approved Social Worker. Under the current legislation in the UK, the Approved Social Worker decides whether an application for compulsory detention in hospital ought to be made and whether detention in hospital is, taking into account all the circumstances, the most appropriate way of providing the care and treatment which the person needs. The proposed reforms allow the application to be made by a suitably trained mental health professional, controversially reverting to the sole involvement of clinicians in relation to compulsory treatment (Reforming the Mental Health Act 2000; Fawcett and Karban, 2001).

These policies have highlighted the need for intensive and extensive support for people experiencing mental health difficulties. Attention has been directed towards the need to reduce stigma and the importance of including service users and carers in planning processes. More resources have also been committed, subject to cost-effectiveness and gate-keeping mechanisms. However, within the policy documents a medicalised framework is clearly emphasised and the importance of controlling those assessed as possibly unpredictable or violent and caring for those regarded as vulnerable is continually underlined. Terms such as 'control' and 'care' have become entrenched in the welfare literature and have in turn been vociferously rejected by proponents of more socially oriented models of mental distress (Sayce, 2000). This draws attention to a fundamental inconsistency in New Labour's mental health policy between the promotion of policy frameworks which advocate 'care' and 'control' on the one hand and those which advocate partnership, service user involvement and social inclusion on the other.

Additional contradictions in relation to current policy initiatives are also evident. As highlighted in Chapter 7, with regard to the provision of citizenship rights New Labour is emphasising responsibilities as a prerequisite for the exercise of rights. This makes it difficult for those diagnosed as mentally ill to achieve enduring rights of citizenship because their ability to work and take on the responsibilities of citizenship, as defined by New Labour, will fluctuate.

A further problem area can be associated with the setting of a National Service Framework for Mental Health and the identification and promotion of national standards and competencies. The setting of standards nationally to be delivered locally and monitored externally, with blueprints provided by the National Service Framework, can ensure that previously marginalised areas are better resourced and that good practice standards are maintained. However, it can also serve to exclude those who do not fit service criteria and to discourage locally relevant and innovative forms of provision. Additionally, it can reinforce the view that professionals have to prioritise safeguarding themselves at the expense of meeting the individual needs of service users and carers. An agenda directed towards controlling outcomes does not neatly fit service user involvement.

It is also possible to argue that the policy documents do not sufficiently differentiate between the self-assessed needs of service users and those of carers. As with previous policies in this field, there is an emphasis on carers' views taking precedence over the expressed wishes of individuals diagnosed as mentally ill. Modernising Mental Health Services (DoH, 1998b, 4.50) states:

> Decisions about care and treatment should be a joint endeavour between staff, patients, service users and discussed with carers as well. Carers are partners alongside health and social services in providing care and support to people with mental health problems.

This statement links into debates about the modernising agenda of New Labour and its underlying rationality. The government promotes policies as being modern and rational. There is an emphasis on order and on the rational, linear progression of policy into practice. Service users are located within a clear diagnosis–treatment continuum and are subject to expert–patient relationships. This easily leads to rhetoric about patients being 'informed, involved and empowered' being translated into standardised consultation exercises with service user control and autonomy giving way to bland consumer-satisfaction surveys. Perkins (2000) believes that this results in a narrow focus on illness, with discussions about rights specifically concentrating on which treatments are preferable rather than on broader rights issues linked to citizenship. As highlighted previously, this reflects a dichotomy between New Labour's emphasis on service user involvement and their centralising, performance target-oriented directives. It is clear that the variance between these policy orientations has been insufficiently acknowledged, particularly in the fields of disability and mental health.

Children, young people and mental health

Where do children and young people fit in relation to current debates and the prevailing policy and practice framework introduced by New Labour? It is interesting to note that the government policy document, Modernising Mental Health Services (DoH, 1998b), and the National Service Framework for Mental Health (2000) have both specifically excluded services for children and adolescents. Services for this group are currently provided by CAMHS. As highlighted, the government proposed an extension of CAMHS in the Green Paper 'Every Child Matters' (2003). Extra funding was also made available by means of CAMHS Innovation Grant Projects. These were awarded to twenty-four project areas in 1998–1999. However, budgets were not ring-fenced and this led to some areas being able to maintain and develop more extensive and integrated services than others, resulting in post-code inequality.

The introduction of CAMHS in the 1990s has been seen by many professionals to have brought about improvements in mental health services for children and young people (Kurtz, 2003). Prior to the 1990s, services for children and young people diagnosed as having mental health problems were characterised by regional variation, a complete lack of standardisation and by the largely uncoordinated involvement of a number of different agencies. Some areas had Child Guidance Clinics, others had a child psychiatrist attached to a psychiatric wing in a General Hospital and some had practically no provision at all. CAMHS introduced a four-tiered approach to problem identification and intervention. Tier One represents the non-specialist primary level where a range of practitioners (for example, general practitioners, health visitors and social workers) identify children and young people with mental health problems at an early stage and offer general advice and, where appropriate, treatment for less severe problems. Tier One also includes a preventative element. Tier Two involves a network of professionals, including child clinical psychologists, child psychiatrists, paediatricians, community psychiatric nurses and educational psychologists. These professionals offer training and consultation to other professionals, a consultation service to families and engage in outreach activities. They also undertake specific assessments. Tier Three is for those children and young people experiencing mental health difficulties diagnosed as complex, persistent and severe. At this level, specialist multi-disciplinary teams assess and treat children and young people, assess for referral to Tier Four, offer consultations and training to other professionals and engage in research activities. Tier Four refers to specialist provision which may be offered at a regional level. It can include specialist outpatient teams, day units and adolescent inpatient units for those diagnosed as severely mentally ill or at risk of suicide, secure forensic adolescent units, eating disorder units and specialist teams for neuro-psychiatric problems (Department of Health, 1995).

However, although the overall CAMHS policy framework is in place, practice varies widely. So too does the allocation of resources. As highlighted in the introduction, CAMHS continues to be uncoordinated, poorly networked, with a lack of standardisation in relation to referral criteria and intervention strategies (Young Minds, 2000a: p. 7; Kurtz, 2003). For example, some agencies refuse to consider a referral if drugs or alcohol are involved (Young Minds, 2000a). Some regard 'challenging behaviour' as being within the remit of CAMHS, others regard it as being outside. There is wide divergence about which difficulties constitute a mental health emergency and which do not. There is also considerable variation in the age of transition between children's and adult services, with some effecting the transition at 16 and some at 19. Recommended improvements include calls for better co-ordination of services, more specialist 'inpatient' provision, the strengthening of specialist community-based services and the inclusion of children and young people with mental health problems within the National Service Framework for Mental Health (Young Minds, 2000a; The Mental Health Foundation, 2001).

However, important though the recommendations highlighted above are, the extent to which they address significant underlying issues remains debatable. It is also unclear whether the changes to CAMHS proposed in 'Every Child Matters' (2003) significantly altered the nature of the services provided or the disparities in provision. As argued in the introduction, mental health policy towards adults can be seen to have a clear relevance for children and young people. Accordingly, the implications warrant exploration. Key features of this approach include the continued use of a predominantly medicalised framework, the introduction of a National Service Framework, and issues of rights and the potential for conflict between children, young people and their parents. These areas will now be reviewed.

Medicalised perspectives

It is clear that discussions focusing on the mental health of children and young people remain firmly positioned within medicalised orientations. As highlighted earlier, medicalised discourses view problems with mental health as illnesses which require specialist diagnosis and treatment. There are positive factors related to medicalised perspectives. These can provide structured frameworks which can enable a person (and their family) not to feel that what is happening to them is their fault. An individual is not seen as responsible for their actions; there are services and professionals to call upon to intervene to provide relief for families, and medication and therapeutic forms of relief are available to 'the patient'. Policies, services and resources can also be directed towards an identified, vulnerable group who require intervention.

However, there are also negative factors. As Bracken and Thomas (2001) highlight, medicalised approaches which focus exclusively on symptoms can result in possible reasons for disturbed behaviour and the contexts in which it is manifested remaining unexplored:

> ...most psychiatric diagnoses are nothing more than a particular way of formulating and naming a person's problems....Psychiatric diagnosis is often little more than a simplification of a complex reality, and by formulating an individual's experiences in terms of pathology it can be profoundly disempowering and stigmatising (Bracken and Thomas, 2001, p. 19).

User or survivor movements have rejected the notion that there is an objective, value-free diagnostic process which moves straightforwardly through a symptom–diagnosis–treatment–cure–continuum. The work of Fernando (1991, 1995, 2002), Rogers and Pilgrim (2003), Sayce (2000) and Bracken and Thomas (2001), to name but a few, have highlighted that unacknowledged cultural, social, economic and ideological assumptions and value systems render any claims to objectivity obsolete. From an historical perspective, a review of nineteenth-century concepts of psychiatry, particularly in relation to how these refer to women, highlights how relative 'facts' can be. An example mentioned in Showalter (1987) shows how Henry Maudsley, the eminent Victorian psychiatrist and professor, both reflected and promoted the view, portrayed as fact, that educational prowess in women affected their menstrual cycle and resulted in serious illnesses.

Beresford (2001) has called for 'non-medicalised alternatives' for children and criticises 'an outmoded psychiatric system that still frequently fails to see the person and only sees the illness'. He goes on to say that current practices miss 'both people's strengths and their difficulties' (Beresford, 2001, p. 14). In discussions about an individual's personhood, issues of gender and ethnicity become particularly pertinent. In this context, it is important to note that women appear in mental health statistics more frequently than men (Prior, 1999). In contrast, in relation to children and adolescents, boys appear more frequently than girls (Social Trends, 2002). Additionally, as has been frequently reported, young African-Caribbean men are over-represented in relation to the diagnosis of psychotic disorders (Rogers and Pilgrim, 2003). The explanations put forward for the above have ranged from the effects of adverse socio-economic factors to the application of stigmatising psychiatric constructs (Fernando, 1991; Barnes and Maple, 1992; Busfield, 1996; Fernando *et al.*, 1998; Pilgrim and Rogers, 1999; Prior, 1999; Fernando, 2002). In relation to Asian women, where medical distress can be presented in physical terms, Pilgrim and Rogers (1999) point to the dangers posed by western psychiatric positivism. They note that mental distress presented as a physical symptom can legitimate a form of medical management where doctors diagnose and treat an underlying mental illness. This, they assert, effects a neat division between physical and mental illness and assumes that the linguistic expression of emotions is transculturally stable. They also maintain that the identification of a pattern with associated treatments serves to discount diversity and to promote responses linked to stereotypical assumptions.

Gender and ethnicity remain under-researched areas with regard to children, young people and the arena of mental health. The issues raised above are pertinent in three key respects. Firstly, they have implications for the collection and analysis of statistics about the overall incidence of mental health difficulties. The apparent increase in the numbers of children and young people who appear to be experiencing mental health problems has resulted in calls for the publication of regular reports on the scale of the mental health problems among children and young people (Young Minds, 2000b). However, statistics on this issue are not transparent 'facts' and require continued interrogation. Secondly, as indicated, more research is needed in relation to gender and ethnicity. Thirdly, there are clearly different ways of explaining the reasons for mental distress, ranging from an emphasis on social causation to a focus on social constructionist perspectives. An example here relates to the identification and prevalence of mental health disorders according to the social class of the father. According to Kurtz (1996), children and young people from social class five (unskilled) are three times more likely to be diagnosed with mental health problems than those in social class one. Reasons given for this can variously emphasise the increased stress experienced by those living in relative poverty in inner-city areas and the likelihood of professionals being more willing to construct/diagnose difficulties as mental health problems for those living in inner cities. In this context, assumptions about ethnicity and gender can significantly influence how a child or young person is viewed and responded to by professionals and agencies. There are also dangers from attempts to identify homogenising patterns which result in standardised responses and which downplay differences.

Pilgrim and Rogers (1999) point to the importance of taking into account the relationship between agency and structure as well as meaning and context when reviewing understandings of mental health. Viewing mental health problems as social facts, although useful in terms of indicating the social origins of mental health problems, presents a unidimensional perspective which constrains developments in the fields of policy and practice. How children are viewed relates to the perspective or perspectives adopted by professionals, parents and peers and these will differ and be influenced by a variety of factors. While this does not deny that some children and young people experience severe mental health difficulties and require professional help, it does draw attention to the dangers of a child or young person becoming *the* condition or *the* problem. Similarly, there is a danger that a predominant focus on one way of responding to a particular difficulty can slip into becoming *the* right and *the* only response.

The implications of a National Service Framework

The incorporation of CAMHS into the National Service Framework for Children, an increase in the resources allocated to CAMHS and the standardisation and co-ordination of provision are strongly supported by professionals, organisations and pressure groups and are part of the modernising drive of New Labour. Currently, in relation to children and young people, similar difficulties can be directed to a variety of agencies and professionals and can be responded to in a range of different ways. The same problem can, for example, be directed towards a social services department, a voluntary agency, the police, the courts, the education services, general practitioners, psychologists or psychiatrists. In each instance, a different response can be obtained. The introduction of a National Service Framework is viewed by the government as a means of matching problems to agencies more consistently. The linking of service performance to national standards by means of 'benchmarking' criteria and the introduction at a national level of professional competencies are also regarded as a way of addressing regional variation and the fragmentation of services. The government is also keen for resources to follow specified target areas and, as has been seen in relation to 'looked after children', some gains have been made. However, as highlighted in Chapter 1, targeting can render the development of a holistic approach to the lives of children and young people, and the variety of contexts in which their lives are lived, problematic. Regional responses to localised areas of need also become a casualty of standardisation.

Moreover, particularly in relation to children and young people, it has to be recognised that the introduction of a National Service Framework and the expansion of CAMHS cannot simply iron out discrepancies related to problem identification and diverse responses. To illustrate this point more fully, an area has to be initially identified as a problem by a child, young person, family, professional or school to warrant action. In this context, it has to be appreciated that girls, boys and concerned others will view and manage similar problems very differently. Some will see themselves in crisis and require emergency intervention, some will seek assistance and some will deny and/or manage the problem or difficulty themselves. Even with the introduction of a National Service Framework, professional responses will continue to differ in relation to conceptualisations of the difficulty being experienced, situational factors, available resources and the level of severity with which a problem is viewed. For example, there will continue to be wide variation in terms of when a difficulty or problem becomes a condition: when high levels of activity in a child becomes a hyperkinetic disorder; when challenging behaviour becomes a conduct disorder; and when a child, having an imaginary friend, is seen to 'hear voices'. In relation to this latter example, hearing voices could be diagnosed as early onset of schizophrenia or, in accordance with the work of Escher *et al.* (1998), interpreted as controlled voice hearing. Additionally, the influence of gender and ethnicity and social, economic and cultural contexts cannot be overemphasised.

Issues of rights and the potential for conflict

A few studies have actually asked children and young people what they want from mental health services. Two key studies which have concentrated on the voices of children and young people in the 16–25-year age group are those carried out by The Mental Health Foundation and reported upon in 1999 and 2001. The Mental Health Foundation Report, published in 2001 and entitled 'Turned Upside Down' (Smith and Leon, 2001, quoted in The Mental Health Foundation, 2001), found that young people feel intimidated by psychiatrists and largely find general practitioners unhelpful. In the study which informed the report, the views of 45 young women and men with experience of mental health crises were explored using questionnaires, face-to-face interviews and focus groups. The majority of those who participated were young women and just under half were from black ethnic minority communities. They talked about not being listened to, about not being heard and supported and about having to meet tightly defined criteria which excluded many of them from seeking help (The Mental Health Foundation, 2001, p. 30). Those involved in the study emphasised the importance of services being able to:

- listen to and understand young people;
- allow and encourage young people to talk and explain their situation;

- provide help and advice;
- be respectful of their situation;
- employ a range of staff with experience of mental health problems;
- facilitate and provide support groups;
- offer confidentiality; and
- involve young people.

The evaluation of the twenty-four CAMHS Innovation Grant Projects (Kurtz, 2003; Kurtz and James, 2003) has also drawn attention to the ways in which creative approaches to the engagement of disaffected young people and the provision of flexible and skilled responses to the needs of children and young people can be linked to positive outcomes.

Research findings highlight the importance of building trust, maintaining confidentiality and of professionals and support workers actively engaging with a child or young person and focusing on self-definitions of problem areas. However, this can raise concerns relating to 'what if' scenarios. 'What if', for example, the child or young person is out of control? 'What if' they are likely to harm themselves? 'What if' they are likely to harm others? 'What if' they have already harmed themselves and/or others? In these situations, placing emphasis on working with the child's/young person's definition of the situation can be regarded as a high-risk strategy. Moreover, research shows that professionals consistently experience difficulties in working with those diagnosed as experiencing moderate to severe mental health problems because these young people refuse to engage in therapeutic or support programmes (Kurtz *et al.*, 1995; Howarth and Street, 2000; Young Minds, 2000a). For some young people, unless those operating in the field of child and adolescent mental health services appropriately engage with the child/young person in a way that they understand, focus on what they think is happening – even if this differs substantially from the professional assessment – and what (if anything) they want to do about it, little is going to be achieved. Research reviewed by Featherstone and Parton (2001) in relation to child protection is relevant here. The authors noted that: 'The child protection system as it currently operates does not appear to be invested in by those whom it is set up to protect' (Featherstone and Parton, Working Paper, p. 25). They point to the very different understandings of the term 'safe' held by adults (parents and professionals), children and young people. For adults, 'safe' means parents/professionals acting in a way which they believe to be in the child or young person's best interests. However, young people associate the term 'safe' with assurances of confidentiality and with the young person maintaining control over what happens to them. For young people, this means confiding in peers, not adults, if there is a fear of losing control over events. The recognition of such widely divergent perspectives between young people and adults can be seen to have a strong relevance for child and adolescent mental health services.

New Labour and the mental health of children and young people

As highlighted, research currently portrays CAMHS as being in crisis (Young Minds, 2000a; The Mental Health Foundation, 2001). Despite placing emphasis on evidence-based practice, New Labour appears not to have taken on board evidence from studies reporting the views of children and young people. There also persists in this area, as with disabled children, a reluctance to consider or involve children outside the parent/child relationship.

A focus on the views of children and young people should be especially important in an area such as mental health, where linking outcomes to intervention strategies is not easy and where performance criteria are hard to determine. However, children and young people with mental health problems, until the publication of 'Every Child Matters' (2003) at least, were not a group to have been significantly targeted by the government. 'Quality Protects', Connexions and the improvements made in CAMHS services in specific areas have made a difference, but clearly problems remain at all levels.

In terms of how services could be developed, there are a range of issues. These include: whether there should be a continuation and extension of current services, but with increased resources and targeting (as outlined in 'Every Child Matters', 2003); whether within service provision there ought to be a shift to a more pronounced social orientation, or whether emphasis should be placed on a flexible, accessible, young person-centred approach. Within such debates, one cannot merely pose a simplistic dichotomy between, for example, social and medical orientations. It is necessary to deconstruct and reconstruct terms such as 'children and young person centred', 'involvement', 'participation' and 'multi-disciplinary'. As part of the deconstructive process, the ways in which these terms are currently used in varying contexts need to be explored and the implications for the different participants or stakeholders require examination. Part of the reconstruction could include the formulation of clear principles upon which services could be based. These principles in turn would need to be frequently reviewed by children, advocates, young people and the other participants involved in service planning and service delivery to prevent fixed, rigid interpretations which over time could subvert their very purpose.

With regard to the policies being promoted by New Labour, there are a range of options which do not appear to have been explored. As highlighted, rather than build on user-based evidence or developmental innovation, there is a tendency for increased resources to be used to provide more of the same, with an enhanced emphasis on rather simplistically defined identification, referral and tracking mechanisms.

In this context, it is clear that, in line with the principles high-lighted above, a range of services could be developed and existing services built upon in relation to what children and young people say they want and would find useful. According to existing research, this would include a wide range of community-oriented, fully resourced, user-friendly services. The Mental Health Foundation (2001) reports that children and young people want directly accessible, non-clinical, confidential, flexible, non-compulsory services available on a 24-hour basis. Interestingly, those young people involved in the research projects place emphasis on such services being staffed by those who have personally experienced similar mental health problems. E-mail and Internet services also feature, as do easily accessible confidential counselling services and independent advocacy services. Full information and publicity for all services is also recommended. Where a child or young person is experiencing very severe or constantly recurring crises, supported access to user-friendly, intensive support services is seen as a progressive way forward. All services would require ongoing 'action evaluations' by all those involved (see Fawcett, 2000), in order to ensure that the services continue to develop and operate in line with what children and young people find helpful.

An additional point to consider relates to the contention that there should be clear differentiation between the involvement of children and young people and that services should develop differently to meet the needs of these two diverse groupings. The situation with regard to younger children is contentious and the case for the involvement of an independent advocate can be clearly made. However, it can be argued that in terms of the development of key principles and accessible supportive, flexible services, similar points can be made for both children and young people.

Conclusion

Changes are taking place in relation to service user involvements and the exercise of autonomy and control with regard to adult services. As Roberts (2000) asserts, the disability movement, with its emphasis on overcoming social, economic and political barriers to the achievement of full-inclusive citizenship rights and eschewing pathologising and objectifying classifications, has influenced survivor movements two decades younger. However, it is important to point out that although disabled people have been involved in writing the Disability Discrimination Act 1995 in the UK and the United Nations Standard Rules and the Declaration of Rights of Disabled Persons, 'survivors' of the mental health system have not been involved in the reform of the Mental Health Act (1983) in the UK (Bracken and Thomas, 2001; Roberts, 2000). Also, under New Labour, priority continues to be given to the protection of the public at the expense of the rights of the individual experiencing mental health difficulties and their claims to inclusive citizenship.

In this chapter, it has been argued that understandings of mental health and policy and practice directives relating to adults determine the context in which policies and practices for children and young people are both devised and implemented. The continued location of mental health provision within a predominantly medicalised framework, the introduction of a National Service Framework, and issues of rights and the potential for conflict between children, young people and their parents have been seen to carry with them a range of implications. Current debates on mental health policy reform provide an opportunity to radically overhaul existing policies and practices and to develop initiatives and projects that are responsive to the stated needs of those concerned. At present, such projects, initiatives and debates continue to operate largely outside the state sector and remain underdeveloped by New Labour.

CHAPTER 9

Children as Carers

Introduction

The 2001 Census revealed that there are approximately 5.2 million people who carry out significant 'caring' responsibilities in England and Wales. Of these, 21 per cent provide 'care' for more than 50 hours per week, 11 per cent for between 20 and 49 hours and 68 per cent for up to 19 hours per week (Census, 2001). With regard to those under 18 who perform caring duties for a family member, conservative estimates place the numbers at over 50,000 (DoH website, 2003). In recent decades, successive governments have been keen to support informal carers, since the provision of informal as opposed to formal 'care' represents considerable savings to local and central government budgets. As a result, over the past 20 years there has been a shift in the position of 'carers'. They have moved from being an unacknowledged diverse grouping of people providing 'care' in the home to an influential group with whom successive governments have been keen to develop informal partnerships.

Along with paid work being promoted by New Labour as a key means of ensuring social inclusion, particularly for those who would otherwise be dependent on benefits, there is an increased expectation that personal caring, either for children or family members, is fitted around paid employment. We have already seen that this can create considerable tensions for a wide range of individuals. For children who occupy 'caring' roles, there is also a disparity in policy and practice between services which focus on children as 'carers' and those which support and enhance the parenting role of disabled parents. This chapter explores such issues, examines the potential impact of New Labour's policies, and considers contemporary practice relating to this heterogeneous grouping of children and young people.

Notions of 'care' and definitions of 'young carers'

An important starting point is the need to interrogate and unpack that simple, yet loaded, term 'care'. Since the late 1970s, this subject has been an area of focus within feminist literature. Finch and Groves (1983), for example, maintained that care in the community equated to care by women. While the assumption that caring is carried out predominantly by women was subsequently challenged by Green in 1988, on the basis of OPCS information, it is clear that women still tend to outnumber men in relation to general caring duties (Social Trends, 2002).

In everyday usage, 'care' can be seen to have a number of different meanings. It can refer to having a form of regard for another, or it can be used to denote strong feelings held about an issue or situation. It can also be used to denote the giving of physical assistance. In this context, the term 'care' is frequently used to refer to input from formal support services or a 'care worker', such as in the statement: 'I receive "care" in the morning to help me get out of bed'. With regard to children and young people, informal 'caring' activities can include a combination of practical tasks, physical care, emotional labour, emotional involvement and additional family duties such as looking after siblings. These 'caring' activities in turn take place within a context of different levels of 'caring' relationships. The overall impact of caring responsibilities upon a child or young person will vary enormously. Although there is little research in this area, it is clear that, as with adult caring, gender and gendered expectations play a part. So too do cultural factors. Dearden and Becker (1995) point to the co-residence of a child in a family with care-giving needs as being more important than gender with regard to a 'young carer' taking on caring responsibilities. However, available statistics show that more girls than boys are likely to be engaged in caring activities and that 14 per cent of 'young carers' come from black and minority ethnic groups (Baldwin and Hurst, 2002). Moreover, the assistance available from statutory services to 'young carers' from minority ethnic communities appears to be poor; a study by Shah and Hatton (1999) found that support was of a very low level and based on unfounded stereotypical assumptions about the care provided by extended families.

It has also to be borne in mind that the title of 'young carer' is, in itself, contentious. This term is being used in this chapter to refer to those under 18 who take on 'caring' responsibilities towards another family member. However, as will be seen later in this chapter, there are a number of different ways in which this diverse grouping of children and young people can be constructed and the very title 'young carer' can be associated with one of these perspectives. It therefore needs to be emphasised that the use of this term as a form of description does not signify acceptance of this particular orientation.

'Young carers' and the legislative context

Although there is no legislation which specifically focuses on 'young carers', there are three key Acts which include relevant provision. These Acts are The Children Act 1989, The Carers (Recognition and Services) Act 1995 and The Carers and Disabled Children Act 2000. All can be seen to insufficiently address the position of 'young carers'. With regard to The Children Act (1989), the SSI Guidance CI(95)12 states that:

> Many young people carry out a level of caring responsibilities which prevents them from enjoying normal social opportunities and from achieving full school attendance. Many 'young carers' with significant caring responsibilities should therefore be seen as 'children in need'.

However, being assessed as a 'child in need' is not a straightforward or transparent process. In order for this to happen, contact has to be made with a social services department and the young person's 'caring' responsibilities have to be regarded as 'significant'. As far as the legislation is concerned, there is no clear definition of the term 'significant'. Interpretations have been drawn from guidance, which focus on whether the caring responsibilities are appropriate, given the age of the young person (LAC (96) 7), and whether the 'care' provided is 'regular and substantial' (The Carers [Recognition and Services] Act 1995). Interpretations of what constitutes 'age appropriate' and/or 'regular and substantial care' will vary within and between social services departments and will inevitably be linked to the availability of resources. If a young person achieves recognition as a 'child in need', then the social services department has a general duty to safeguard and promote their welfare and to provide those services which are seen to be appropriate.

The Carers (Recognition and Services) Act 1995 includes provision for children and young people under 18 who provide or intend to provide a substantial amount of care on a regular basis. This Act represented a considerable breakthrough at the time and followed media publicity about the plight of 'young carers'. The Act entitles 'carers', including 'young carers', to request an assessment of their ability to provide and to continue to provide care at the time when an assessment, reassessment or review is being carried out of the person requiring 'care'. It obliges the social services department to take into account the result of the 'carer's' assessment when making decisions about the services to be provided. It does not, however, direct the social services department to provide services.

The Carers and Disabled Children Act (2000) strengthens The Carers (Recognition and Services) Act 1995. Under this legislation, a young person has the right to an assessment of their ability to provide and to continue to provide 'care' even if the person they 'care for' refuses to have their own care needs assessed. Following an assessment, a 'young carer' is entitled to receive those services that they have been assessed as needing in order to enable them to care or to continue to care for the person requiring care. However, charges can be attached to the provision of such services. The Act also entitles carers to receive direct payments and vouchers for respite or short-term breaks. These provisions address the needs of 'young carers' more fully than previously. However, in practice there remain dilemmas. One example is where a parent refuses an assessment. Although the young person is entitled to their own assessment, such a refusal by a parent or family member would place the young carer in a very difficult position and would constitute a considerable barrier. The possibility of being charged for the services provided could constitute yet another hurdle, since it could be the person requiring 'care' or another family member who would have to pay the charge.

With regard to the operation of the current legislation, there are issues relating to how child care and adult services teams liaise to provide combined assessments and to co-ordinate services so that both the welfare of the 'young carer' and the 'caring' demands placed upon them are simultaneously addressed. In addition, there are emotional and psychological barriers which families can erect which militate against the seeking of outside help. However, despite obvious problems, there have been many positive initiatives for 'young carers' undertaken by statutory and voluntary services.

Investing in children and young people as carers

In a review of research findings on the impact of caring responsibilities on children, Baldwin and Hurst (2002) emphasise the ways in which caring can have positive effects for young people and can contribute to the acquisition of skills and attributes such as maturity, responsibility, decision-making and personal and practical skills. However, there are also potential adverse effects. A recent study funded by the Joseph Rowntree Foundation (2000), for example, notes that children who operate as 'carers' frequently miss schooling and are more likely to suffer poverty and social isolation than their peers. Although many are mature for their years, with a wide range of practical skills and experiences, they also often lack formal qualifications. This in turn can limit opportunities in adulthood, either by persuading the young person that continuing to care for a family member is a sensible option or by restricting their employment opportunities to those available in the caring services.

New Labour has initiated a number of general policy initiatives, which, although not targeted on 'young carers', have the potential to bring constructive benefits. The Connexions initiative, for example, which relates to the 13–19-year-old age group, focuses on the importance of ensuring that all young people are allocated a personal advisor to help with information, advice and support and to facilitate access to specialist services if required. Although this initiative was originally intended to be targeted on those excluded from school or those who were experiencing difficulties, the revised universal application has changed the emphasis to one which focuses on careers and education rather than problems. In turn, the QP programme aims to improve the situation of all 'children in need' and, again, has the potential to support 'young carers'. However, the ways in which provision has either been targeted or has a wider-ranging application draws attention to potential problem areas for 'young carers'. When provision is targeted, it can be difficult to ensure that statutory agencies are able to identify 'young carers' and to provide the forms of support necessary to meet the needs of both the child and the parents in the particular family context. When provision is more generalised, the possibilities of stigma resulting from participation in such a scheme are minimised, but the issue of the scheme becoming so broad that its effectiveness is diluted for groups such as 'young carers', whose support needs could be considerable, is brought to the fore.

The contested position of 'young carers'

Becker *et al.* (1998) refer to four perspectives which inform strategies for supporting 'young carers' and their families. These orientations derive from the medical literature, from the social model of disability, from the 'young carers' literature, and from a paradigm which they refer to as the 'family perspective'. With regard to whether New Labour promotes one perspective more than another, one can say that New Labour, as noted, has not particularly targeted this group for attention, but in relation to the general measures introduced, such as Connexions and QP, there appears to be a tendency to adopt the analysis of the 'young carers' literature. This can be seen by means of the inclusion of this grouping within the 'children in need' framework and the ways in which young carers have been incorporated within the Department of Health's Carers website. However, it is important to point out that onus has also been placed on the Social Services Inspectorate to look at the ways in which disabled adults can be supported in their parenting role (DoH website, 2003).

With regard to the four perspectives, the medical orientation tends to focus on the clinical condition and the effects of this on the family. An individualising, pathologising and categorising approach evident in this literature in this 1970s resulted in the formulation of the social model of disability which was defined from the outset in terms of binary opposition to medicalised conceptualisations. Since the emergence of the social model of disability in the early 1970s, the debate has moved on and the influence of the social model on medicalised understandings and practices has been significant. However, there do remain clear differences in emphasis. Medicalised approaches tend to focus on treatment, rehabilitation and 'care' and the problems associated with these areas for the individual and the family, including 'young carers'. Social model proponents eschew the continued individualising emphasis and call for positive social, political, economic and cultural solutions to socially constructed problems (for example, Hales, 1996; Oliver, 1996; Barnes *et al.*, 1999). Accordingly, rather than emphasis being placed on how significant caring duties can have a negative and restrictive impact on a young person's childhood, advocates of the social model of disability recommend that emphasis should be placed on the ways in which those requiring personal assistance and their families are multiply-disadvantaged, excluded and oppressed.

The 'young carers' literature has developed the identification of this group of children and young people from the 1980s onwards. It has focused on the problems associated with defining a young carer, identifying their characteristics and assessing the overall numbers of children and young people engaged in 'caring' activities. There has also been an emphasis on the roles and responsibilities placed on 'young carers' and the overall impact of caring (Meredith, 1991; Parker, 1992; Aldridge and Becker, 1994; Mahon and Higgins, 1995; Becker *et al.*, 1998). There have been debates within this literature about whether 'young carers' effectively engage in forms of role reversal with their parents. However, Parker (1995) refutes such claims. She counters stereotypical assumptions that requiring 'care' equals the adoption of a dependent position by the parent. In this context, she distinguishes between parenting which involves concern for the child's welfare and parental activity which relates to the tasks that parents undertake as parents. Parker (1995) maintains that although having an impairment may affect parental activity, it will not alter parenting as she defines it.

The work of the Young Carers Research Group at Loughborough University has played a central role in contributing to the literature on 'young carers'. Orientations drawn from this literature stress that a social model perspective, which focuses on what should be available, cannot ignore the situation of those affected by current service deficiencies. In relation to the arguments put forward by proponents of the social model of disability that children should not be providing care in the community, with the concomitant restrictions on their lives, the 'young carers' perspective places emphasis on a certain acceptance of current realities. It maintains that the provision of comprehensive support services for disabled parents and their children, although eminently desirable, could not totally prevent children from having to take on caring responsibilities since there would always be those who have been socialised into caring roles to consider. Although supporting the provision of full supportive and comprehensive services, they also doubt whether these would be available in all cases.

Becker *et al.* (1998), building on the 'young carers' literature and social model of disability perspectives, advocate the adoption of a 'family perspective'. They see this as a means of combining both the practices and the conclusions of both orientations. The 'family perspective' focuses on a 'young carer's' rights as a child and as a 'carer' but does not exclude or prioritise these over the rights of their disabled parents. They assert that this approach emerged as a direct consequence of the debate between the rights of disabled people and the rights of children who 'care' and maintain that this perspective 'is congruent with the principle of the government's refocusing strategy which emphasises prevention in a family context as opposed to protection' (Becker *et al.*, 1998, p. 52; see also Chapter 4).

The 'family perspective' is promoted as the way forward in relation to the provision of support services for 'young carers' and their families. Becker *et al.* (1998) build on the 'young carers' perspective and insist that children who operate as 'carers' have needs which must be both acknowledged and addressed and assert that young caring is inevitable in that chronic parental illness and disability cannot be avoided. They also maintain that it is impossible to ensure that welfare organisations and professionals always operate in an empowering and demand-led way. Accordingly, they argue that the 'family perspective', which stresses the importance of family autonomy and family rights, is in the best interest of 'young carers' and their families.

The 'family perspective' clearly views children and young people with caring responsibilities as 'young carers' with rights. Advocates of this approach specifically highlight the importance of the right to assessment and to support, advocacy, information and counselling services. The right to be included in family discussions about needs, assessments, service provision and the rehabilitative programmes for their parents is also prioritised, along with the right of a young carer to continue or to stop caring if this is what they and their families want.

Proponents of the 'family perspective' relate practice considerations to current legislation and highlight examples of good practice from 'young carers' projects, family centres and Department of Health guidance. They advocate support for 'young carers' being placed in the context of the whole family and support the holistic approach to family intervention and the assessment process contained in the Framework for the Assessment of Children in Need and their Families (2000). They recommend an increase in the provision of 'young carers' projects and the use of family centres. However, they also give prominence to research findings which clearly demonstrate that the fear of what will happen following professional intervention is one of the biggest factors deterring families from making contact with service providers (Meredith, 1991; Aldridge and Becker, 1994; Becker *et al.*, 1998). They state that intervention at the point of assessment must be 'positive, non-threatening and sensitively managed' and exhort professionals and agencies to encourage and facilitate a positive response to families in need of support (Aldridge and Becker, 1994, pp. 64–65). They also acknowledge the preference of 'young carers' and their families to seek information, support and assistance from the voluntary sector in the UK. Accordingly, the importance of striking the 'right' balance between the prevention of child caring activities and the provision of interventionist strategies to determine and address needs is highlighted.

Ways forward which have been promoted both in the UK and in the international context by proponents of the 'family perspective' include strengthening the rights of 'young carers', raising awareness by introducing specifically oriented training and development programmes and generating effective multi-agency support and case monitoring systems. Additionally, there are calls for more research on the numbers of young carers and on patterns of care giving to establish and maintain a database to inform policy and practice. Hantrais and Becker (1995) maintain that the 1989 UN Convention on the Rights of the Child could aid the development of a cross-national framework for both securing the rights of 'young carers' and operate as a yardstick to measure international policy and service developments.

The implications for children and young people

All the orientations discussed above position the 'young carer' differently. Medicalised perspectives concentrate on the disabled person and on treating the impairment and/or organising rehabilitative/ supportive services. In line with this orientation, 'young carers' feature as part of family and informal support networks. In this context, their needs are variously identified, assessed and addressed as part of prevailing health and social services operating procedures. The 'young carers' literature builds and reorients this perspective by naming, defining and enumerating 'the problem'. 'Young carers' are seen to have needs and rights which the public and government have to specifically address.

However, proponents of the social model of disability believe that both the 'young carers' and the 'family perspective' lose sight of how 'young carers' have been socially constructed and appropriated. Morris (1996) makes it clear that rather than acknowledge inevitable service failures, it is the right of the child not to perform caring tasks and that it is the role of the state to ensure that appropriate services are provided. She regards the social construction of 'young carers' as a further example of the barriers confronting disabled parents, particularly lone disabled female parents. Morris gives voice to the fear of disabled mothers that not only will available services fail to meet their needs but that their children will be seen to be overburdened with caring responsibilities and will need to be 'rescued from' the 'burden' of disability and caring.

The 'family perspective' can be seen to focus attention on constructive developments. Accordingly, this orientation fully acknowledges the importance of responding to the situation of a child or young person in the context of their family, environment and personal support systems. The utility of taking full account of cultural, financial and social circumstances is also stressed. However, the 'family perspective' can also be seen to include constraining factors. An emphasis on 'the family' can fail to differentiate between different wants, expectations and support needs, and can gloss over the context of an individual's life and the full interplay of family relationships, especially power relationships. We have already noted that looking at children and young people almost exclusively in the context of their family can lead to a restrictive and narrow focus. Children and young people can be seen to be influenced by peers and by a whole network of relationships outside of the family. In terms of attending to quality of life matters, these external associations are important and warrant greater recognition.

The 'family perspective' importantly places emphasis on the expressed wants of 'young carers' for recognition, information, practical support and someone to talk to (Social Services Inspectorate, 1995). However, perhaps there is insufficient recognition that assessment procedures may in practice fail to engage with such needs for a variety of reasons. As noted in Chapter 7, the possibility of a request for assistance triggering an assessment process which could be regarded as unnecessarily invasive needs to be taken on board.

There is also the debate about prevention and intervention to consider. The argument about whether a responsibility to intervene to meet the needs of 'young carers' dilutes the responsibility to ensure appropriate and adequate services for disabled adults to obviate the need for 'young carers' to 'care' is a pertinent one. It has a certain circularity which proponents of the 'family perspective' have sought to address by focusing on the here and now. However, the strength of their arguments, particularly with regard to advocates of disability rights perspectives, as highlighted, is particularly contentious as it is seen to legitimise continued deficiencies in services to adults.

Finally, debates have emerged in relation to whether the onus for seeking support should be left to the child/young person and/or their family or whether professionals operating in both the voluntary and the statutory sectors should take responsibility for both identifying and responding to the expressed and perceived needs of 'young carers'. Baldwin and Hurst (2002), in relation to both these areas, draw attention to the dangers of young carers being 'locked' into caring roles by increased support being provided to them rather than to their disabled parents and by the provision of intrusive or expensive services which cause families to reject what is on offer and to continue to rely on their children.

Conclusion

As discussed, New Labour has not addressed the needs of 'young carers' specifically, although changes to 'carers' legislation has recognised their needs, and, as 'children in need', they are included in existing children's legislation and in more generalised initiatives. However, this very emphasis on 'young carers' as 'children in need' rather than as children or young people with rights, as we have seen, has the potential to draw attention to their needs rather than to address those of disabled parents.

As emphasised by advocates of the social model of disability, the recognition and provision of support for 'young carers' should not be presented as a trade-off for the lack of adequate services for disabled parents. However, the existence of 'young carers' can be acknowledged without, at the same time, negating the claims of disabled parents. With regard to provision for 'young carers', this can encompass a range of easily accessible options. These include acknowledging the importance of a supportive, non-threatening approach with dedicated projects, secure funding and committed advisory groups. 'Young carers' have emphasised the utility of advice, support services and access to information via the Internet and independent advocacy services. Emotional support and counselling services which take self-referrals have similarly been regarded as useful forms of assistance (Becker *et al.*, 1998). It is also important to draw attention to the valuable work undertaken by those who co-ordinate and network across agencies and professions and who build alliances between the statutory and voluntary sectors. It is notable that the most valued support comes from voluntary sector projects. Baldwin and Hurst (2002) estimate that in 2001 there were nearly 150 voluntary projects with each project serving between 70 and 100 'young carers'. However, these projects cater for only one in three of the possible 50,000 young people heavily involved in providing care.

Informal carers save the government millions of pounds per year. The important role they play is increasingly being recognised, although not necessarily properly funded. The recognition of 'young carers' has served to give a name to a valuable family resource and arguably a socially constructed conscript to the ranks of 'carers'. The role that they play and the implications for individuals will vary according to the interaction of age, gender, ethnicity, family composition and family circumstances. Such roles will also alter over time and reflect changing circumstances. New Labour's declared intention is to ensure that the policies of social inclusion have a practical relevance for all. It remains to be seen how their policies will, in the longer term, impact on this heterogeneous collection of children and young people.

CHAPTER 10

Conclusions

Introduction

Having examined recent policy developments in relation to a wide range of child welfare issues, this chapter offers some conclusions with respect to the significance of these developments. Since 1997, UK central government has shown considerable commitment to intervening in the lives of children in a variety of ways and to a much greater degree than previous administrations. Interventions in relation to specific categories of children sit alongside broader initiatives in relation to children generally, such as those concerned with abolishing child poverty. In one sense, the simple expansion of government interest in child welfare policy is the most significant development. Within a social investment strategy, this is not surprising, since such an approach ensures that 'the child in particular takes on an iconic status' (Lister, 2003, p. 437).

Earlier in the book, we sought to outline the core constituents of New Labour's policy rationale. This reflects our main motive in writing the book, which was to seek to provide a guide, assessment and overview of recent developments for those who have struggled to keep pace with Labour's activism in child welfare. A further reason for our examination of this area was our consciousness of the increasing importance of child welfare issues to a range of different audiences. Child protection, youth justice and looked after children have been policy concerns for decades, but these have now been joined – particularly since the 1989 Children Act – by a cluster of growing concerns over children and mental health, children and disability, and children as carers. However, the priorities of government have proved to be very different from those of policy activists and researchers. Recently, policy change has focused strongly on some of these areas and much less so on others.

Once we have considered how the policy changes we have examined relate to the development of a social investment state, we discuss more detailed conclusions in three broad areas. The first of these concerns developments with regard to children's rights to involvement and participation in decision-making. Secondly, we consider recent approaches to family support and to the wider role of parents; particularly the state's approach to relationships between parents and children. Thirdly, we consider the changing role of the state with respect to intervening in family life and providing policy frameworks within which a range of professions and institutions (such as local authorities and voluntary sector bodies) now have to work.

Social exclusion/social investment

New Labour entered office with strong rhetoric about the need to tackle social exclusion. In interrogating that rhetoric, we have found writings on the social investment state to be of considerable value. Such writings have helped us to understand how and why New Labour has moved towards a progressively more targeted approach to child welfare in the last 20 years, from a generalised focus on social justice and inequality centred on social class and family, through a narrower focus on social exclusion and now to a more utilitarian focus on social investment.

From this perspective, certain groups, such as young offenders, young children in disadvantaged areas and looked after children, represent significant opportunities (of reduced crime, improved cognitive and behavioural development and more productive involvement in the paid labour force respectively) and threats (more crime, long-term disaffection and disadvantage and a range of forms of social exclusion respectively). Other groups, such as disabled children, are perceived to be more easily controlled by their families, their schools and other social agencies and to present less of an external threat to social cohesion. This argument is summarised in Figure 10.1.

Under New Labour, considerable benefits have accrued to children. It is worth remembering that under the post-war welfare state, children's concerns were often neglected. However, the more targeted focus which flows from a social investment rationale is problematic in a number of respects. First, it produces a hyperactivism in those areas which are singled out for intervention. This can make

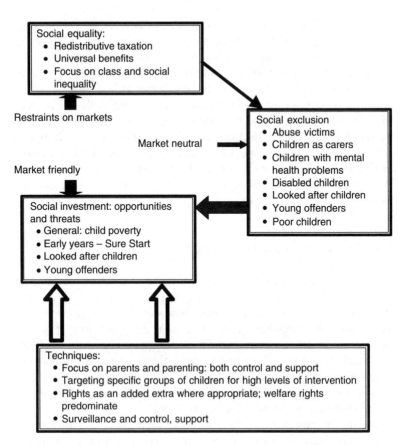

Figure 10.1   New Labour, children and the social investment state

the wealth of initiatives – in areas such as child poverty, youth justice and looked after children – exhausting and confusing. Secondly, there is an inequity involved. Comparing levels of social exclusion is invidious, but it would be hard to argue that many children with disabilities, mental health problems or acting as young carers are less excluded than looked after children. However, the latter group has received much higher levels of government attention. Also, New Labour has not fully grasped the implications of its work-focused strategy; for example, with respect to disabled children. The same problem applies to education, where disabled children continue to suffer from exclusionary practices.

In 2003, the appointment of a Minister for Children and Young People and Labour's Green Paper on 'Children at Risk' suggested that governmental interest in child welfare services of various kinds will remain high for the foreseeable future and there will be no let-up in the level of initiatives in this field. One particular feature of that development, the move of significant parts of child welfare policy to the Department for Education and Skills, demonstrates the continued dominance of future employment issues in government thinking.

However, it is important to acknowledge that government policies in relation to children cannot be read exclusively in terms of a social investment rationale. For example, the goal of abolishing child poverty builds on the concerns of equality, exclusion *and* investment approaches. Furthermore, whilst we consider the social investment state thesis key to understanding why there is a relatively low level of interest in certain groups of children and stronger interest in others, other factors – ministerial interest, the research base, the current role of parents and the role of campaigning bodies – also play a significant part.

Children's rights, involvement and autonomy

It is clear that New Labour has had a strong interest in both articulating and supporting children's rights to protection, economic support and social resources. As we saw in Chapters 3 and 5 especially, initiatives such as Sure Start and QP mark a significant departure from the approach of recent Conservative administrations.

New Labour has clearly been less concerned with promoting 'children's rights' in the sense of participation and involvement, with the main exception to this being the case of looked after children. However, in this area the promotion of children's rights to participation and involvement – while wholly laudable and sometimes imaginatively implemented at a local level (Robbins, 2001) – is based on a protectionist rationale that is explicitly linked to the various institutional abuse inquiries of the 1990s. This means that its strong focus on involvement and participation does not hold implications for other child welfare policy areas. For example, young children, such as those in Sure Start programmes, are not consulted about services whereas older children, under Children's Fund initiatives, are consulted. Also, the proactivity of children is largely ignored with respect to the wider child protection system, which remains adult-dominated (see Chapter 4). In short, there has been no paradigm shift with respect to the involvement of children in decision-making; New Labour still operates with a developmental model of childhood.

Labour's more general paternalism (in two senses; both its support for State involvement and its support for greater parental involvement in the lives of children) contrasts with its reluctance to intervene in general terms in the relationships between parents and children – except in the sense of 'supporting' the parental task. The most stark illustration of this is the failure to criminalise the physical punishment of children by their parents. There is a welcome interest in supporting, but also a somewhat more contentious interest in prioritising, the parent–child role. In some cases, as in youth justice, support for parents slips quite explicitly into coercion. The government is primarily interested in supporting children as members of families rather than as individuals in their own right. This is particularly apparent with regard to disabled children, children who operate as carers and children with mental health problems.

New Labour exhibits an uneasiness about participatory rights claims generally, sharing the Conservative analysis that 'excessive' focus on rights tends to fragment society. Coupling rights with responsibilities is a feature of one-nation Conservatism and, indeed, Labour has traditionally exhibited a similar authoritarian streak on many social issues (the liberalism of Roy Jenkins when Home Secretary in the 1960s, for example, standing out as distinctly exceptional in Labour Party history). However, it would be misleading and simplistic to deny that New Labour has certainly provided a more welcome environment in which debates about the rights and autonomy of children can take place. The establishment of the Children and Young Person's unit and its obvious commitment to consultation with young people from all walks of life is both an implicit recognition of this logic and an important step forward in this regard. So too is the belated acknowledgement of the need for a Children's Commissioner for England.

New Labour's approach to parents

Central to New Labour's project of managing welfare policy more efficiently and rationally are attempts to recruit parents to their strategy. Just as children have become more important to adults on an emotional level, as sources of stability and connection, so has parenting itself become more important to government as a source of stability in providing effective support for children in a changing world. However, as we have indicated, parents are viewed – and hence treated – ambiguously. Certain groups of parents are actively targeted for particular measures and increased funding. The task of 'parenting' itself is the core concern, rather than parents as such, because of a pragmatic understanding that concepts of 'family' and actual families are too unstable and complex for simplistic support or control strategies. That is not to say that there are not active attempts to reconstruct a version of ideal family practices. Such a model of concerned parenting is made most explicit in the approaches to looked after children, particularly in the central elements of the Children (Leaving Care) Act. Indeed, within 'Supporting Families: A Consultation Document', the preferred family model appears suspiciously like Blair's own: conjugal, heterosexual parents, both involved in the paid workforce, living with all of their birth children. However, this is too particular a version to encompass the wide variety of practices and is therefore not reinforced by general policy measures. Even Labour's adoption White Paper, whilst stressing its support for extending to more children 'the kind of loving family life which most of us take for granted' (Department of Health, 2002b, p. 3), studiously avoided being more prescriptive than this.

The role of the state

At a national level, Labour has largely followed trends in central government management of social welfare services that began under the Conservatives. If anything, it has magnified and intensified these. In recent years, a New Public Management focus on results, target-setting and performance measurement has been driven forward with a new sense of purpose. This has largely been with the intention of seeking to preserve and develop the public sector by making it as goal-oriented as the private sector. It is a more thorough and systematic attempt at John Major's goal of moving away from Thatcherite attacks on the public sector by seeking to improve its delivery. However, the 'Citizens' Charter' model which Major developed was a rather weak affair when compared to New Labour's systems of central control. A particular feature of this approach has been the expansion of cross-departmental policy initiatives – dissolving the boundaries between government departments in order to develop problem-based approaches rather than departmentally based policies. The involvement of the Home Office in family policy from 1997 is one aspect of this. So too is the joint working and joint guidance issued by government in relation to both child assessment and the education of looked after children. However, developments in 2003, with the enhancement of the role of the Department for Education and Skills, raise the possibility of a return to a departmentally based approach to child welfare.

Labour's hyperactivity on control, monitoring and target-setting can be viewed as a compensation for its lack of interest in tackling the basic structures of social welfare policy inherited from the Conservatives. Thus far, it has balanced the extra pressures it has put on local government, in particular, with extra resources. Nonetheless, the pressures it has brought to bear on agencies in the public sector – and not just those delivering services to children – have been considerable and while extra funds have minimised resistance, they have not compensated for the exhaustion and confusion often experienced as one set of initiatives, zones, targets, standards and performance indicators follows quickly on the heels of the previous set.

An area of continuity with the Conservatives which is worthy of note is that Labour has been willing to be highly and publicly critical of the past performance of local government in delivering services to children. This criticism is presented in technocratic, managerialist terms and often makes little reference to social structure, major social divisions and specific contexts. Increasing centralisation also makes it difficult for local services to demonstrate local accountability and prioritise locally identified problem areas.

In contrast, for areas of work not subject to such target-setting, workers and communities may experience constraints in service provision. One example from the experience of one of the authors is provided by the work of Health Action Zone projects in Bradford. Although communities have welcomed the extra input and have valued specifically targeted projects which have focused, for example, on children excluded from school and mental health projects, they have continued to draw attention to public health issues such as rats and rubbish in local areas. In this context, the lack of resources available to local government to be spent on basic infrastructure activities continues to contribute towards negative perceptions of public services (Henderson and Torn, 2002). Moreover, target-setting in one area may conflict with the achievement of targets in other areas (Tunstill, 2000).

Conclusion

Whatever 'final' results emerge, New Labour's reforms will have made it the most interventionist and radical with respect to child welfare policy for many decades. In this book, we have explored both *what* has been done and *why*. We would contend that the developments we have been tracing mark a strong reorientation of child welfare policy towards support for long-term economic success within a global economy. Therefore, New Labour has focused on those areas where intervention is most relevant to this long-term objective. There is ample evidence that this has brought considerable benefits to many children and throughout this book we have documented such benefits.

However, there are costs. There is a greater use of regulation and surveillance of both parents and children. Also, the instrumental nature of the discourse around investment does not do justice to the complexities of children's lives and identities. The overwhelming focus on parents as the dominant source of support for children can be argued to narrow horizons and neglect alternative visions of childhood. Finally, the focus on achieving good outcomes for children runs the risk of focusing much more on the responsibilities of parents than on their support needs.

References

Abbott, D., Morris, J. and Ward, L. (2000) *Disabled Children and Residential Schools: A Survey of Local Authority Policy and Practice, Bristol*. Bristol: Norah Fry Research Centre, University of Bristol.

Adams, R. (2002) *Social Policy for Social Work*. Basingstoke: Palgrave.

Alanen, L. (1988) 'Rethinking childhood', *Acta Sociologica*, 31, pp. 53–67.

Aldridge, J. and Becker, S. (1994) *My Child, My Carer: The Parents' Perspective*. Loughborough: Young Carers Research Group, Loughborough University.

Archard, D. (1993) *Children: Rights and Childhood*. London: Routledge.

Audit Commission (1996) *Misspent Youth... Young People and Crime*. London: Audit Commission.

Audit Commission (1998) *Misspent Youth '98: The Challenge for Youth Justice*. Abingdon: Audit Commission Publications.

Baldwin, S. and Hurst, M. (2002) 'Children as carers', in Bradshaw, J. (ed.) *The Well-being of Children in the UK*. London: Save the Children/University of York.

Ball, M. (1998) *Disabled Children: Directions for Their Future Care*. London: Department of Health in association with the SSI and the Council for Disabled Children.

Barnes, C. and Mercer, G. (1996) (eds) *Exploring the Divide: Illness and Disability*. Leeds: The Disability Press.

Barnes, C., Mercer, G. and Shakespeare, T. (1999) *Exploring Disability: A Sociological Introduction*. Cambridge: Polity Press.

Barnes, M. (2003) Presentation to the Social Policy Association Annual Conference 17 July 2003, University of Middlesbrough.

Barnes, M. and Maple, N. (1992) *Women and Mental Health: Challenging the Stereotypes*. Birmingham: Venture Press.

Bartlett, J. (1994) *Will you be Mother?* London: Virago.

Barton, and Oliver, (1997) *Disability Studies: Past, Present and Future*. Leeds: The Disability Press.

BBC News Tuesday 12 March 2002 http://news.bbc.co.uk/hi/english/health/newsid1867000/1867410stm.

Bebbington, A. and Miles, J. (1989) 'The background of children who enter local authority care', *British Journal of Social Work*, 19(5), pp. 249–269.

Beck, U. and Beck-Gernsheim, E. (1995) *The Normal Chaos of Love*. Cambridge: Polity.

Becker, S., Aldridge, J. and Dearden, C. (1998) *Young Carers and Their Families*. Oxford: Blackwell.

Benn, M. (1998) *Madonna and Child: Towards a New Politics of Motherhood*. London: Jonathan Cape.

Benyon, J. and Edwards, E. (1997) 'Understanding less, condemning more? conservative law and order, 1979–1997'. Paper presented at the Political Studies Association Annual Conference, University of Ulster, 8–10 April.

Beresford, B. (1994) *Caring for a Severely Disabled Child*. York: Social Policy Research Unit.

Beresford, P. (2001) 'Removing the pain', *Community Care*, 7–13 June, p. 14.

Beresford, B., Sloper, P., Baldwin, S. and Newman, T. (1996) *What Works in Services for Families with a Disabled Child*. Barkinside: Barnardos.

Berridge, D. and Brodie, I. (1998) *Children's Homes Revisited*. London: Jessica Kingsley.

Biehal, N., Clayden, J., Stein, M. and Wade, J. (1995) *Moving On: Young People and Leaving Care Schemes*. London: HMSO.

Björnberg, U. (2002) 'Ideology and choice between work and care', *Critical Social Policy*, 22(1), pp. 33–53.

Blair, T. (1996) *New Britain: My Vision of a Young Country*. London: 4th Estate.

Blair, T. (1998) *The Third Way: New Politics for the New Century*. (Fabian Pamphlet 588). London: Fabian Society.

Blair, T. (1999) *Beveridge Lecture*, March, London.

Bowling, B. and Phillips, C. (2002) *Racism, Crime and Justice*. London: Harlow.

Bracken, P. and Thomas, P. (2001) 'Evidence-based medicine and advocacy', *Openmind*, 107, January–February, p. 19.

Bradshaw, J. (2002) 'Comparisons of child poverty and deprivation internationally', in Bradshaw, J. (ed.) *The Well-being of Children in the UK*. York: University of York, Save the Children.

Bradshaw, J. (2003) 'Poor children', *Children & Society Special Issue*, 17(3), pp. 173–184.

Brandwein, R. (ed.) (1999) *Battered Women, Children and Welfare Reform*. London/ Thousand Oaks, Sage.

Brannen, J. (1999) 'Reconsidering children and childhood: sociological and policy perspectives', in Silva, E. B. and Smart, C. (eds) *The New Family?* London: Sage.

Braye, S. (2000) 'Participation and involvement in social care: an overview', in Kemshall, H. and Littlechild, R. (eds) *User Involvement and Participation in Social Care: Research Informing Practice*. London: Jessica Kingsley, pp. 9–28.

Britton, L., Chatrik, B., Coles, R. and Craig, G. (2002) *Missing Connexions*. York: J. R. Rowntree Foundation.

Broad, B. (1998) *Young People Leaving Care: Life After the Children Act 1989*. London: Jessica Kingsley.

Broad, B. (2003) *After the Act: Implementing the Children (Leaving Care) Act 2000*. Leicester: De Montfort University.

Busfield, J. (1996) *Men, Women and Madness: Understanding Gender and Mental Disorder*. London: Macmillan.

Butler, I. and Williamson, H. (1994) *Children Speak: Children, Trauma and Social Work*. London: Longman/NSPCC.

Calder, A. (2000) 'Financial support for care leavers', *Poverty*, 106, pp. 11–13.

Callinicos, A. (2001) *Against the Third Way*. Cambridge: Polity.

Campbell, B. (1988) *Unofficial Secrets, Child Sexual Abuse: The Cleveland Case*. London: Virago.

Campbell, S. (2002) 'Implementing Anti-social Behaviour Orders: messages for practitioners', in *Findings: 160*. London: Home Office Research and Statistics Directorate.

Cawson, P., Wattam, C., Brooker, C. and Kelly, G. (2000) *Child Maltreatment in the United Kingdom*. London: NSPCC.

Census (2001) Office of Population, Census and Surveys 2001. London: The Stationery Office.

Charman, S. and Savage, S. (2002) 'Toughing it out: New Labour's criminal record', in Powell, M. (ed.) *Evaluating New Labour's Welfare Reforms*. Bristol: The Policy Press, pp. 211–229.

Chief Secretary to the Treasury (2003) *Every Child Matters*. (Cm 5860). London: The Stationery Office.

Children and Society (2002) *Special Issue. Children as Social Actors: The ESRC Children 5–16 Programme*, 16(2).

Clarke, J., Langan, M. and Williams, F. (2000) 'The construction of the British Welfare State 1945–1975', in Cochrane, A., Clarke, J. and Gewirtz, S. (eds) *Comparing Welfare States* (2nd Edition). London: Sage, in association with The Open University.

Coates, D. and Lawler, P. (eds) (2000) *New Labour in Power*. Manchester: Manchester University Press.

Coleman, J. and Schofield, J. (2001) *Key Data on Adolescence*. Brighton: Trust for the Study of Adolescence.

Coles, B. and Maile, S. (2002) 'Children, young people and crime', in Bradshaw, J. (ed.) *The Well-being of Children in the UK*. London: Save the Children, pp. 288–302.

Corby, B. (2002) 'Child abuse and child protection', in Goldson, B., Lavallette, M. and McKechnie, J. (eds) *Children, Welfare and the State*. London: Sage.

Corker, M. and French, S. (1999) *Disability Discourse*. Buckingham: Open University Press.

Corsaro, W. A. (1997) *The Sociology of Childhood*. Thousand Oaks: Sage.

Coward, R. (1993) *Our Treacherous Hearts: Why Women Let Men Get Their Way*. London: Faber and Faber.

Coward, R. (1999) *Sacred Cows*. London: Harper Collins.

Craig, G. (2001) 'Social exclusion: is labour working?', *Community Care*, 27 September–3 October, pp. 40–41.

Crewe, I., Day, N. and Fox, A. (1991) *The British Electorate: 1963–1987*. Cambridge: Cambridge University Press.

Cunningham, H. (1995) *Children and Childhood in Western Society Since 1500*. London: Longman.

Dale, P., Davies, M., Morrison, T. and Waters, J. (1986) *Dangerous Families: Assessment and Treatment of Child Abuse*. London: Tavistock.

Daniel, P. and Ivatts, J. (1998) *Children and Social Policy*. London: Palgrave Macmillan.

Dean, M. (2002) 'Don't ignore the flexible parent', *The Guardian*, 11 December.

Dearden, C. and Becker, S. (1995) *Young Carers: The Facts*. Sutton: Reed Business Publishing.

Department for Education and Employment (1994) *The Code of Practice on the Identification and Assessment of Special Educational Needs*. London: HMSO.

Department for Education and Skills (2003a) The SEN Action Programme (Consultation Document). London: DfES.

Department for Education and Skills (2003b) *Every Child Matters* (Cm 5860). London: The Stationery office.

Department of Health (1989) *An Introduction to The Children Act 1989*. London: HMSO.

Department of Health (1991a) *The Children Act 1989 Guidance and Regulations: Volume 2, Family Support, Day Care and Educational Provision for Young Children.* London: HMSO.

Department of Health (1991b) *The Children Act 1989 Guidance and Regulations: Volume 4, Residential Care.* London: The Stationery Office.

Department of Health (1995) *Child Protection: Messages from Research.* London: The Stationery Office.

Department of Health (1998a) *Modernising Social Services.* London: The Stationery Office.

Department of Health (1998b) *Modernising Mental Health Services.* London: The Stationery Office.

Department of Health (1999a) LAC(99)33 *The Quality Protects Programme 2001/02 Transforming Children's Services.*

Department of Health (1999b) *Me, Survive? Out There? New Arrangements for Young People Living in and Leaving Care.* London: Department of Health.

Department of Health (2000a) *Framework for the Assessment of Children in Need and Their Families.* London: The Stationery Office.

Department of Health (2000b) *Framework for the Assessment of Children in Need and Their Families the Assessment Framework Practice Guidance Questionnaires and Scales Assessment Recording Forms.* London: The Stationery Office.

Department of Health (2000c) *The Children Act Report, 1995–1999.* Norwich: The Stationery Office.

Department of Health (2000d) *Learning the Lessons: The Government's Response to 'Lost in Care'* (Cm 4776). London: The Stationery Office.

Department of Health (2001a) *Studies Informing the Framework for the Assessment of Children in Need and Their Families.* London: The Stationery Office.

Department of Health (2001b) *The Children Act Now: Messages from Research.* London: The Stationery Office.

Department of Health (2001c) *Children (Leaving Care) Act 2000: Regulations and Guidance.* London: The Stationery Office.

Department of Health (2001d) *The Valuing People White Paper.* London: The Stationery Office.

Department of Health (2001e) *Listening, Hearing and Responding: Core Principles for the Involvement of Children.* London: The Stationery Office.

Department of Health (2002a) *Children Looked After in England: 2001/2002.* London: National Statistics/Department of Health.

Department of Health (2002b) *Adoption: A New Approach* (Cm 5017). London: The Stationery Office.

Department of Health (2003a) 'Care Leavers, year ending 31 March 2002, England', London: Department of Health Statistical Bulletin.

Department of Health (2003b) *Assessing Children's Needs and Circumstances: The Impact of the Assessment Framework.* London: DH.

DoH website (2003) www.doh.gov.uk.

Department of Health (2004) *Draft Disability Bill.* London: Department of Health.

Department of Health and Department for Education and Employment (2000) *Guidance on the Education of Children and Young People in Public Care.* London: Department of Health, Department for Education and Employment.

Department of Health, Home Office, Department for Education and Employment (1999) *Working Together to Safeguard Children in Need and Their Families.* London: The Stationery Office.

Department of Health and Social Security (1988) *Report of the Inquiry into Child Abuse in Cleveland*. London: HMSO.

Department of Trade and Industry (2001) *Work and Parents: Competitiveness and Choice.*

Disability Rights Commission (2002) *Survey of Young Disabled People Aged 16–24.* London: DRC Research and Evaluation Unit.

Dobson, A. (2001) 'Exclusion still the norm for young disabled people', *Community Care*, 6–12 September, 2001, pp. 10–11.

Donzelot, J. (1980) *The Policing of Families*. London: Hutchinson.

Drake, R. F. (1999) *Understanding Disability Policies*. Basingstoke: Macmillan.

Drakeford, M. and Vanstone, M. (2000) 'Social exclusion and the politics of criminal justice: a tale of two administrations', *The Howard Journal*, 39(4), pp. 369–381.

Draper, L. (2001) 'Being evaluated: a practitioner's view', *Children and Society*, 15, pp. 46–52.

Driver, S. and Martell, S. (2002) *Blair's Britain*. Cambridge: Polity.

Duncan, S. and Edwards, R. (1999) *Lone Mothers, Paid Work and Gendered Moral Rationalities*. Basingstoke: Macmillan.

Dunn, J. and Deater-Deckard, K. (2001) *Children's Views of their Changing Families.* York: Joseph Rowntree.

Escher, S., Romme, M. and Buiks, A. (1998) 'Small take – voice hearing in children', *Open Mind*, 92, July/August. pp. 12–13.

Esping-Andersen, G. (ed.) (2002) *Why We Need a New Welfare State*. Oxford: Oxford University Press.

Fairclough, N. (2000) *New Labour New Language*. London: Routledge.

Fawcett, B. (2000) *Feminist Perspectives on Disability*. Harlow: Prentice Hall.

Fawcett, B. and Karban, K. (2001) *Social Work and Mental Health: The End or a New Beginning*, unpublished.

Featherstone, B. (1997) 'I wouldn't do your job: women, social work and child abuse', in Hollway, W. and Featherstone, B. (eds) *Mothering and Ambivalence*. London: Routledge.

Featherstone, B. (2002) 'Gender and child abuse', in Stewart, K.I. and James, A. (eds) *The Handbook of Child Protection* (2nd Edition). Harcourt: Bailliere Tindall.

Featherstone, B. (2003) 'Taking Fathers Seriously', *British Journal of Social Work*, 33, pp. 239–254.

Featherstone, B. and Parton N. (2001) *Placing Children Centrally in Child Protection*. Unpublished. University of Huddersfield.

Featherstone, B., Fawcett, B. and Goddard, J. (2002) 'New Labour, children's rights and the United Nations: "could do better"', *Journal of Social Welfare and Family Law*, 24(4), pp. 475–484.

Ferguson, H. (2001) 'Social work, individualization and life politics', *British Journal of Social Work*, 31, pp. 41–55.

Fernando, S. (1991) *Mental Health, Race and Culture*. Basingstoke: Macmillan/Mind.

Fernando, S. (1995) *Mental Health in a Multi-ethnic Society – A Multi-disciplinary Handbook*. London: Routledge.

Fernando, S. (2002) *Mental Health, Race and Culture, Second Edition*. Basingstoke: Palgrave.

Fernando, S., Ndegwa, D. and Wilson, M. (1998) *Forensic Psychiatry, Race and Culture*. London: Routledge.

Finch, J. (1989) *Family Obligations and Social Change*. Cambridge: Polity Press.

First Key (2001) *Policy Briefing: The Draft Children (Leaving Care) Regulations and Guidance 2001*. Leeds: First Key.

Fortin, J. (2002a) 'The Human Rights Act 1998: human rights for children too', in Franklin, B. (ed.) *The New Handbook of Children's Rights: Comparative Policy and Practice*. London: Routledge, pp. 119–135.

Fortin, J. (2002b) 'Children's rights and the impact of two international conventions: The UNCRC and the ECHR', in Thorpe, Rt Hon Lord Justice and Cowton, C. (eds) *Delight and Dole: The Children Act Ten Years On*. Bristol: Jordan Publishing.

Fox Harding, L. (1991) *Perspectives in Child Care Policy*. Harlow: Longman.

Fox Harding, L. (1996) *Family, State and Social Policy*. Basingstoke: Macmillan.

Fox Harding, L. (1997) *Perspectives on Child Care Policy* (2nd Edition). Harlow: Longman.

Fox Harding, L. (1999) '"Family values" and Conservative government policy', in Jagger, G. and Wright, C. (eds) *Changing family values*. London: Routledge.

Franklin, B. (ed.) (2002) *The New Handbook of Children's Rights: Comparative Policy and Practice*. London: Routledge.

Freely, M. (1996) *What About Us? An Open Letter to the Mothers Feminism Forgot*. London: Bloomsbury.

Freely, M. (2000) *The Parent Trap: Children, Families and the New Morality*. London: Virago.

Freeman, M. (1993) 'Laws, conventions and rights', *Children & Society*, 7(1), pp. 37–48.

Freeman, M. (ed.) (1996) *Children's Rights: A Comparative Perspective*. Aldershot: Dartmouth.

Freeman, M. (2002) 'Children's rights ten years after ratification', in Franklin, B. (ed.) *The New Handbook of Children's Rights: Comparative Policy and Practice*. London: Routledge, pp. 100–118.

Frosh, S. (2002) 'Characteristics of sexual abusers', in Stewart, K. and James, A. (eds) *The Handbook of Child Protection* (2nd Edition). Harcourt: Bailliere Tindall.

Frost, N. and Featherstone, B. (2003) 'Families, social change and diversity', in Bell, M. and Stewart, K. (eds) *The Practitioner's Guide to Working with Families*. Bastingstoke: Palgrave.

Frost, N. and Stein, M. (1989) *The Politics of Child Welfare*. London: Harvester Wheatsheaf.

Frost, N., Mills, S. and Stein, M. (1999) *Understanding Residential Child Care*. Vermont, USA: Ashgate.

Gamble, A. (1988) *The Free Economy and the Strong State: The Politics of Thatcherism*. Basingstoke: Macmillan Education.

Gardner, R. (2002) *Supporting Families: Protecting Children in the Community*. Chickester: Wiley/NSPCC.

Garrett, P. (2002) 'Encounters in the new welfare domains of the Third Way: social work, the Connexions agency and personal advisers', *Critical Social Policy*, 22(4), pp. 596–619.

Ghate, D. and Ramalla, M. (2002) *Positive Parenting: The National Evaluation of the Youth Justice Board's Parenting Programme*. London: Youth Justice Board Policy Research Bureau.

Ghazi, P. (2003) *The 24 hour Family: A Parent's Guide to the Work-Life Balance*. London: The Women's Press.

Giddens, A. (1992) *The Transformation of Intimacy*. Cambridge: Polity.

Giddens, A. (1998) *The Third Way: The Renewal of Social Democracy*. Cambridge: Polity Press.

Giddens, A. (2002) *Where Now for New Labour?* Cambridge: Fabian Society/Polity Press.

Gilligan, R. (1997) 'Beyond permanence? The importance of resilience in child placement practice and planning', *Adoption and Fostering*, 21, pp. 12–20.

Gilligan, R. (2000) *Promoting Resilience: A Resource Guide on Working with Children in the Care System*. London: BAAF.

Goddard, J. (2000) Research review: the education of looked after children, *Child and Family Social Work*, 5(1), pp. 79–86.

Goddard, J. (2001) 'Children (Leaving Care) Act 2000: a commentary', *Welfare Benefits*, 8(3), pp. 25–34.

Goldson, B. (ed.) (2000) *The New Youth Justice*. Lyme Regis: Russell House Publishing.

Goldson, B. (2001) 'The demonization of children: from the symbolic to the institutional', in Foley, J., Roche, J. and Tucker, S. (eds) *Children in Society: Contemporary Theory, Policy and Practice*. Basingstoke: Palgrave, pp. 34–41.

Goldson, B. (2002) 'Children, crime and the state', in Goldson, B., Lavalette, M. and McKechnie, J. (eds) *Children, Welfare and the State*. London: Sage.

Gordon, L. (1989) *Heroes of Their Own Lives*. London: Virago.

Green, H. (1988) *Informal Carers: General Household Survey 1985*. London: HMSO.

Gregg, P., Harkness, S. and Machin, S. (1999) 'Poor kids: trends in child poverty in Britain, 1968–96', in *Fiscal Studies*, 20(2), London: Institute of Fiscal Studies.

Hales, G. (ed.) (1996) *Beyond Disability: Towards an Enabling Society*. London: Oxford University Press/Sage.

Hall, S. (2003) 'Blair repeals law to ban smoking', *The Guardian*, 25 June, p. 8.

Hallett, C., Murray, C. and Punch, S. (2003) 'Young people and welfare: negotiating pathways', in Hallett, C. and Prout, A. (eds) *The Voices of Children: Social Policy for a New Century*. London: Routledge Farmer.

Hansard 8 April 1998 House of Commons Debates.

Hansard 15 April 1999 House of Commons Debates.

Hansard 21 June 2000 *Children (Leaving Care) Bill, Second Reading*, House of Commons.

Hantrais, L. and Becker, S. (1995) 'Young carers in Europe: a comparative perspective', in Becker, S. (ed.) *Young Carers in Europe: An Exploratory Cross-national Study in Britain, France, Sweden and Germany*. Loughborough: Young Carers Research Group in association with the European Research Centre, Loughborough University.

Hayden, C., Goddard, J., Gorin, S. and van der Spek, N. (1999) *State Child Care: Looking After Children?* London: Jessica Kingsley.

Hearn, J. (1990) '"Child Abuse" and men's violence', in Violence Against Children Study Group (eds) *Taking Child Abuse Seriously*. London: Routledge.

Heclo, H. (1974) *Social Policy in Britain and Sweden*. New Haven: Yale University Press.

Henderson, J. and Torn, A. (2002) *Neighbourhood Evaluation – Phase One: Study of Twelve Project Teams*. Bradford: Bradford University, Health Action Zone Evaluation Project.

Hendrick, H. (1994) *Child Welfare: 1870–1989*. London: Routledge.

Hendrick, H. (2003) *Child Welfare: Historical Dimensions, Contemporary Debates*. Bristol: Policy Press.

Henricson, C., Coleman, J. and Roker, D. (2000) 'Parenting in the youth justice context', *The Howard Journal*, 39(4), pp. 325–338.

Henricson, C., Katz, I., Mesie, J., Sandison, M. and Tunstill, J. (2001) *National Mapping of Family Services in England and Wales: A Consultation Document*. London: National Family and Parenting Institute.

Henwood, K. (2002) 'Fatherhood and transition to parenthood: findings from a Norfolk Study', ESRC Seminar, University of East Anglia, 12 April.

Herring, J. (2001) *Family Law*. Harlow: Pearson Education.

Hill, M. (1997a) 'Participatory research with children: research review', *Child and Family Social Work*, 2(3), pp. 171–185.

Hill, M. (1997b) 'What children and young people say they want from social services', *Research, Policy and Planning*, 15(3), pp. 17–27.

Hill, M. and Tisdall, K. (1997) *Children and Society*. London: Longman.

Hodgkin, R. (1994) 'Cultural relativism and the UN convention on the rights of the child', *Children and Society*, 8(4), pp. 296–299.

Hollis, V. and Goodman, M. (2003) *Prison Population Briefing, England and Wales*. London: Home Office.

Holman, B. (1988) *Putting Families First*. Basingstoke: Macmillan.

Home Office (1991) *Safer Communities: The Local Delivery of Crime Prevention Through the Partnership Approach*. London: Home Office.

Home Office (1995) *Digest 3: Information on the Criminal Justice System in England and Wales*. London: Home Office Research and Statistics Department.

Home Office (1997a) *Tackling Youth Crime: A Consultation Paper*. London: Home Office.

Home Office (1997b) *No More Excuses – A New Approach to Tackling Youth Crime in England and Wales*. (CM3809). London: The Stationery Office.

Home Office (1998a) *Youth Justice: The Statutory Principle Aim of Preventing Offending by Children and Young People*. London: Home Office.

Home Office (1998b) *Introductory Guide to the Crime and Disorder Act*. London: Home Office.

Home Office (1998c) *Supporting Families: A Consultation Document*. London: The Stationery Office.

Home Office (2000) *Attitudes to Crime and Criminal Justice: Findings from the 1998 British Crime Survey*. London: Home Office.

Home Office (2001) *Criminal Justice: The Way Ahead*. (Cm 5074). London: The Stationery Office.

Home Office (2003a) 'Crime down 9 per cent', Press Release, ref 105/2003, 4 April.

Home Office (2003b) *Youth Justice: The Next Steps*. London: Home Office.

Home Office, Lord Chancellor's Dept, Youth Justice Board (2002) *Referral Orders and Youth Offender Panels: Guidance for Courts, Youth Offending Teams and Youth Offender Panels*. London: Home Office.

Hood, R. and Roddam, A. (2000) 'Crime, sentencing and punishment', in Halsey, A. H. (ed.) with Webb, J. *Twentieth Century British Social Trends*. Basingstoke: Macmillan.

Hooper, C.-A. (2002) 'Maltreatment of children', in Bradshaw, J. (ed.) *The Well-being of Children in the UK*. York: University of York, Save the Children.

House of Commons Education and Employment Select Committee (1998) *Disaffected Children*. London: The Stationery Office.

House of Commons Health Select Committee (1998) *Children Looked After by Local Authorities*. (HC 319–1). London: The Stationery Office.

Howarth, C. and Street, C. (2000) *Sidelined: Young Adults' Access to Services*. London: New Policy Institute.

Howe, G. (1995) *Working with Schizophrenia: A Needs Base Approach*. London: Jessica Kingsley.

Hoyle, C. and Rose, D. (2001) 'Labour, law and order', *The Political Quarterly*, pp. 76–85.

Hutchinson, E.D. and Charlesworth, L. W. (2000) 'Securing the welfare of children: policies past, present and future', *Families in Society*, 81(6), pp. 576–585.

Jackson, S. (1998) *High Achievers: A Study of Young People who have been in Residential or Foster Care*. Final Report to Leverhulme Trust. Swansea: University of Wales.

Jackson, S., Ajayi, S. and Quigley, M. (2003) *By Degrees: The First Year*. London: National Children's Bureau.

James, A. and Prout, A. (1997) *Constructing and Reconstructing Childhood: Contemporary Issues in the Sociological Study of Childhood*. London: Routledge.

James, A., Jenks, C. and Prout, A. (1998) *Theorising Childhood*. Bristol: Polity Press.

James, A. L. and James, A. (2001) 'Tightening the net: children, community and control', *British Journal of Sociology*, 52(2), pp. 211–228.

Jeffery, L. (2003) 'New Labour, new initiatives: Sure Start and the children's fund', in Frost, N., Lloyd, A. and Jeffery, L. (eds) *The RHP Companion to Family Support*. Dorset: Russell House Publishing.

Jeffs, T. (2002) 'Schooling, education and children's rights', in Franklin, B. (ed.) *The New Handbook of Children's Rights: Comparative Policy and Practice*. London: Routledge, pp. 45–59.

Jenks, C. (1996) *Childhood*. London: Routledge.

Jenson, J. and Saint-Martin, D. (2001) 'Changing Citizenship regimes: social policy strategies in the social investment state', workshop on 'Fostering Social Cohesion: A Comparison of New Policy Strategies'. Universite de Montreal, 21–22 June.

John, P. (1998) *Analysing Public Policy*. London: Pinter.

Jones, G. (1995) *Leaving Home*. Buckingham: Open University Press.

Jones, D. (2001) '"Misjudged youth": a critique of the Audit Commission's reports on youth justice', *British Journal of Criminology*, 41, pp. 362–380.

Jordan, B. and Jordan, C. (2000) *Social Work and the Third Way: Tough Love as Social Policy*. London: Sage.

Kamerman, S. and Kahn, A. (eds) (1978) *Family Policy in Fourteen Countries*. New York: University of Columbia Press.

Kaplan, E.-A. (1992) *Motherhood and Representation: The Mother in Popular Culture and Melodrama*. London: Routledge.

Keeping Children Safe (2003) London: The Stationery Office.

Kempe, C. H., Silverman, F. N., Steele, B. F., Droegemuller, W. and Silver, H. K. (1962) 'The Battered Child Syndrome', *Journal of the American Medical Association*, 181, pp. 17–24.

King, A., Denver, D., Maclean, I., Norris, P., Norton, P., Sanders, D. and Seyd, P. (1998) *New Labour Triumphs: Britain at the Polls*. New Jersey: Chatham House Publishers.

Kirkwood, A. (1993) *The Leicestershire Inquiry 1992*. Leicester: Leicestershire Country Council.

Kurtz, Z. (1996) *Treating Children Well*. London: The Mental Health Foundation.

Kurtz, Z. (2003) 'Outcomes for children's health and well-being', *Children & Society*, 17, pp. 173–183.

Kurtz, Z. and James, C. (2003) *What's New: Learning from the CAMHS Innovation Projects*. London: Department of Health.

Kurtz, Z., Thornes, R. and Wolkind, S. (1995) *Services for the Mental Health of Children and Young People in England: Assessment of Needs and Unmet Need*. London: Public Health Directorate, South Thames RHA.

Labour Party (1987) *Labour Manifesto: Britain Will Win*. London: Labour Party.

Labour Party (1992) *Labour's Election Manifesto: It's Time to Get Britain Working Again*. London: Labour Party.

Labour Party (1997) *New Labour: Because Britain Deserves Better*. London: Labour Party.

Labour Party (2001) *Labour's Manifesto 2001: Ambitions for Britain*. London: Labour Party.

Lamb, M. E. (1997) 'Fathers and child development: an introductory overview', in Lamb, M. E. (ed.) *The Role of the Father in Child Development* (3rd Edition). Chichester, Wiley.

Land, H. (1999) 'New Labour, new families', in Dean, H. and Woods, R. (eds) *Social Policy Review, no.11*. Luton: SPA.

Land, H. (2002) *Building on Sand: Facing the Future Policy Papers*. London: Day Care Trust.

Lansdown, G. (2001) 'Children's welfare and children's rights', in Foley, P., Roche, J. and Tucker, S. (eds) *Children in Society: Contemporary Theory, Policy and Practice*. Basingstoke: Palgrave, pp. 87–97.

Lee, N. (2001) *Childhood and Society: Growing Up in an Age of Uncertainty*. Buckingham: Open University Press.

Levy, A. and Kahan, B. (1991) *The Pindown Experience and the Protection of Children*. Stafford: Staffordshire County Council.

Lewis, J. (2001) *The End of Marriage? Individualism and Intimate Relations*. Cheltenham: Edward Elgar.

Lind, C. (2003) 'Stability for children? The Adoption and Children Act 2002', *Journal of Social Welfare and Family Law*, 25(2), pp. 173–188.

Linford Rees, W. L. (1978) *A Short Textbook of Psychiatry* (2nd Edition). London: Hodder and Stoughton.

Lister, R. (1994) '"She has other duties" – women, citizenship and social security', in Baldwin, S. and Fallingham, J. (eds) *Social Security and Social Change*. Hemel Hempstead: Harvester Wheatsheaf.

Lister, R. (2000) 'Gender and social policy', in Clarke, J., Gewirtz, S. and Lewis, G. (eds) *Rethinking Social Policy*. London: Sage/Open University.

Lister, R. (2001) 'New Labour: a study in ambiguity from a position of ambivalence', *Critical Social Policy*, 21(4), pp. 425–449.

Lister, R. (2002) 'Investing in citizen-workers of the future: New Labour's "third way" in welfare reform', Paper for Panel 10555-8FB: Redesigning Welfare Regimes: The Building Blocks of a New Architecture, Annual Meeting of the American Political Association.

Lister, R. (2003) 'Investing in citizen-workers of the future: transformations in citizenship and the state under New Labour', *Social Policy and Administration*, 37(5), pp. 427–443.

Longford, F. (Chair) (1964) *Crime – A Challenge to Us All*. London: Labour Party.

Lord Laming (2003) *The Victoria Climbié Inquiry: Report*. London: TSO.

Lynes, D. and Goddard, J. (1995) *The View from the Front: The User View of Child-Care in Norfolk*. Norwich: Norfolk County Council.

Lyon, C. M. (1997), 'Children Abused Within the Care System', in Parton, N. (ed.) *Child Protection and Family Support: Tensions, Contradictions and Possibilities*. London: Routledge, pp. 126–145.

MacLeod, M. (1999) '"Don't just do it" children's access to help and protection', in Parton, N. and Wattam, C. (eds) *Child Sexual Abuse: Responding to the Experiences of Children*. Chichester: Wiley/NSPCC.

Maguire, M. and Kynch, J. (2000) *Public Perceptions of Victims' Experiences of Victim Support: Findings from the 1998 British Crime Survey*. London: Home Office Research, Development and Statistics Directorate.

Mahon, A. and Higgins, J. (1995) *'A Life of Our Own' – Young Carers: An Evaluation of Three RHA Funded Projects in Merseyside; Appendices; and Summary*. Manchester: Health Services Management Unit.

Mama, A. (1989) 'Violence against Black women: gender, race and state responses', *Feminist Review*, 32, pp. 30–48.

Mann, K. and Roseneil, S. (1999) 'Poor choices? gender, agency and the underclass debate', in Jagger, G. and Wright, C. (eds) *Changing Family Values*. London: Routledge.

Matheson, J. and Babb, P. (eds) (2002) *Social Trends 32*. London: The Stationery Office.

Mattinson, J. and Mirrlees-Black, C. (2000) *Attitudes to Crime and Criminal Justice: Findings from the 1998 British Crime Survey*. London: Home Office.

McRobbie, A. (2000) 'Feminism and the Third Way', *Feminist Review*, 64, pp. 97–112.

Meltzer, H., Gatward, R., Goodman, R. and Ford, T. (2000) *Mental Health of Children and Adolescents in Great Britain: A Survey Carried Out in 1999 by the Social Servey Division of ONS*. London, TSO.

Meredith, H. (1991) 'Young carers: the unacceptable face of community care', *Social Work and Social Sciences Review*, 3(Supplement), pp. 47–51.

Middleton, L. (1999) *Disabled Children: Challenging Social Exclusion*. Oxford: Blackwell Science.

Milligan, C. and Dowie, A. (1998) *What Do Children Need from Their Fathers?* Occasional Paper 42. Edinburgh: University of Edinburgh, Centre for Theology and Public Issues.

Mirrlees-Black, C. (1999) *Domestic Violence Findings: Findings from a New BCS Self-completion questionnaire*. London: Home Office.

Morris, J. (1993) *Pride Against Prejudice*. London: Women's Press.

Morris, J. (1995) *Easy Targets: A Disability Rights Perspective on the 'Young Carers' Debate, Young Carers Something to Think About: Report of Four SSI Workshops, May–July*. London: Social Services Inspectorate, Department of Health.

Morris, J. (1996) *Encounters with Strangers: Feminism and Disability*. London: Women's Press.

Morris, J. (1997) *Gone Missing? A Research and Policy Review of Disabled Children Living Away from Their Families*. London: Who Cares Trust.

Morris, J. (2001) *That Kind of Life*. London: Scope/Community Fund.

Moss, P., Dillon, J. and Statham, J. (2000) 'The "child in need" and the "rich child": discourses, constructions and practices', *Critical Social Policy*, 20(2), pp. 233–255.

Muncie, J. (2002) 'Children's rights and youth justice', in Franklin, B. (ed.) *The New Handbook of Children's Rights: Comparative Policy and Practice*. London: Routledge.

Munro, E. (2001) 'Empowering looked after children', *Child and Family Social Work*, 6, pp. 129–137.

National Care Standards Commission (2002) *Management Statement and Financial Memorandum*. London: NCSC.

National Family and Parenting Institute (2002) *Family Policy Digest 2001–2002*. London: National Family and Parenting Institute.

Newburn, T., Crawford, A., Earle, R., Goldie, S., Hale, C., Hallam, A., Masters, G., Netten, A., Saunders, R., Sharpe, K. and Uglow, S. (2002) *The Introduction of Referral Orders into the Youth Justice System: Final Report*. London: Home Office Research.

Newman, J. (2001) *Modernising Governance, New Labour, Policy and Society*. London: Sage.

NHS Health Advisory Service (1986) *Bridge Over Troubled Waters*. London: HAS.

Oliver, M. (1983) *Social Work with Disabled People*. Basingstoke: Macmillan.

Oliver, M. (1990) *The Politics of Disablement*. Basingstoke: Macmillan.

Oliver, M. (1996) *Understanding Disability: From Theory to Practice*. Basingstoke: Macmillan.

Oliver, M. and Barnes C. (1998) *Disabled People and Social Policy: From Exclusion to Inclusion*. London: Longman.

Olsen, R. (1996) 'Young carers: challenging the facts and politics of research into children and caring', *Disability and Society*, 11(1), pp. 41–54.

O'Sullivan, J. (2001) 'Two weeks paid leave for new dads: a small but symbolic step', *The Independent on Sunday*. 25 March, p. 16.

Oswin, M. (1984) *They Keep Going Away*. London: King Edward Hospital Fund for London.

Oswin, M. (1998) 'A historical perspective', in Robinson, C. and Stalker, K. (eds) *Growing Up with Disability*. London and Philadelphia: Jessica Kingsley.

Pacey, M. (2002) 'Facing the childcare challenge', *Poverty*, 113, www. cpag.org.uk.

Parker, G. (1992) 'Counting care: numbers and types of informal carers', in J. Twigg (ed.) *Carers: Research and Practice*. HMSO: London, pp. 6–29.

Parker, G. (1995) *Contribution to Young Carers; Something to Think About, Report of Four SSI Workshops, May–July*. London: Social Services Inspectorate/Department of Health.

Parker, R. (1997) 'The production of material ambivalence', in Hollway, W. and Featherstone, B. (eds) *Mothering and Ambivalence*. London: Routledge.

Parliamentary Debates (Hansard) Second Reading Debate on Children and Young Person's Bill, Vol. 779 (1968/69), 11.3.69.

Parton, N. (1985) *The Politics of Child Abuse*. Basingstoke: Macmillan.

Parton, N. (1990) 'Taking child abuse seriously', in Violence Against Children Study Group (eds) *Taking Child Abuse Seriously*. London: Unwin Hyman.

Parton, N. (1991) *Governing the Family, Child Care, Child Protection and the State*. Basingstoke: Macmillan.

Parton, N. (1996) 'Child protection, family support and social work: a critical appraisal of the Department of Health research studies in child protection', *Child and Family Social Work*, 1, pp. 3–11.

Parton, N. (2002) 'Protecting children: a socio-historical analysis', in Wilson, K. and James, A. (eds) *The Child Protection Handbook* (2nd Edition), Edinburgh: Harcourt Publishers.

Parton, N. and Wattam, C. (1999) 'Introduction' in *Child Sexual Abuse: Responding to the Experiences of Children*. Chichester: Wiley/NSPCC.

Pascall, G. (1986) *Social Policy: A Feminist Analysis*. London: Routledge.

Peel, J. (1997) 'Talking tough: crime, law and punishment', in Bailey, R. (ed.) *The BBC News General Election Guide*. Glasgow: Harper Collins.

Perkins, R. (1999) 'Madness, distress and the language of inclusion', *Open Mind*, 98, July/August. p. 4.

Perkins, R. (2000) 'I have a vision', *Open Mind*, 104, July/August, p. 6.

Pilgrim, D. and Rogers, A. (1996) *A Sociology of Mental Health and Illness*. Buckingham: Open University Press.

Pilgrim, D. and Rogers, A. (1999) *A Sociology of Mental Health and Illness* (2nd Edition). Buckingham: Open University Press.

Pitts, J. (1988) *The Politics of Juvenile Crime*. London: Sage.

Platt, J. (2000) 'The return of the wheelbarrow men; or, the arrival of postmodern penality?', *British Journal of Criminology*, 40, pp. 127–145.

Police Complaints Authority (1993) *Inquiry into Police Investigations of Complaints of Child and Sexual Abuse in Leicestershire Children's Homes: A Summary*. London: Police Complaints Authority.

Powell, M . (ed.) (2002) *Evaluating New Labour's Welfare Reforms*. Bristol: The Policy Press.

Priestley, M. (1999) 'Transforming disability identity through critical literacy and the cultural politics of language', in Corker, M. and French, S. (eds) *Disability Discourse*. Buckingham: Open University Press.

Prior, L. (1993) *The Social Organisation of Mental Illness*. London: Sage.

Prior, P. M. (1999) *Gender and Mental Health*. Basingstoke: Macmillan.

Pritchard, C. (1992) 'Children's homicide as an indicator of effective child protection: a comparative study of Western European statistics', *British Journal of Social Work*, 22, pp. 663–684.

Prout, A. (2001) 'Researching children as social actors: introduction to the children 5–16 programme', *Children and Society*, 16(2), pp. 67–77.

Pugh, G. (2003) 'Early Childhood Services: Evolution or Resolution?', *Children & Society Special Issue*, 17(3), pp. 184–195.

Read, J. and Clements, L. (2001) *Disabled Children and the Law: Research and Good Practice*. London: Jessica Kingsley.

Reder, P., Duncan, S. and Gray, M. (1993) *Beyond Blame: Child Abuse Tragedies Revisited*. London: Routledge.

Reid, K. (2002) 'Anti-social behaviour orders: some current issues', *Journal of Social Welfare and Family Law*, 24(2), pp. 205–222.

Rentoul, J. (2001) *Tony Blair: Prime Minister*. London: Warner Books.

Report of the Committee of Enquiry into Mental Handicap Nursing and Care (1979) (Jay Report) *CMND 7468*. London: HMSO.

Report of the Committee on Child Health Services (1976) (Court Report) *CMND 6684*. London: HMSO.

Rich, A. (1976) *Of Woman Born: Motherhood as Experience and Institution*. New York, Norton.

Ridge, T. (2002) *Childhood Poverty and Social Exclusion from a Child's Perspective*. Bristol: The Policy Press.

Robbins, D. (2000) *Tracking Progress in Children's Services: An Evaluation of Local Responses to the Quality Protects Programme, Year 2: National Overview Report.* London: Department of Health.

Robbins, D. (2001) *Transforming Children's Services. An Evaluation of Local Responses to the Quality Protects Programme.* London: The Stationery Office.

Roberts, M. (2000) 'Come together? right now?', *Open Mind,* 106, November–December, p. 12.

Roberts, M. (2001) 'Childcare policy', in Foley, P., Roche, J. and Tucker, S. (eds) *Children in Society: Contemporary Theory, Policy and Practice.* Basingstoke: Palgrave/Open University.

Roberts, M. (2003) *Talking Politics,* Radio 4, 2 August.

Roberts Centre (2003) *A Review of the Children Leaving Care Act 2000: Report of a Seminar on 26th November 2002.* London: Roberts Centre.

Roche, J. (1995) 'Children's rights: in the name of the child', *Journal of Social Welfare and Family Law,* 17(3), pp. 281–99.

Roche, J. (2001) 'Making progress', *Community Care,* 1–7 November, pp. 40–41.

Rogers, A. and Pilgrim, D. (2003) *Mental Health and Inequality,* Basingstoke: Palgrave Macmillan.

Russell, P. (1996) Personal Communication, Council for Disabled Children, National Children's Bureau, London.

Ryan, M. (1999) *The Children Act 1989: Putting It into Practice* (2nd Edition). Aldershot: Ashgate.

Sabatier, P. (ed.) (1999) *Theories of the Policy Process.* Boulder: Westview Press.

Sabatier, P. and Jenkins-Smith, H. (1993) *Policy Change and Learning: An Advocacy Coalition Approach.* Boulder: Westview Press.

Sayce, L. (2000) *From Psychiatric Patient to Citizen: Overcoming Discrimination and Social Exclusion.* Basingstoke: Macmillan.

Scourfield, J. and Drakeford, M. (2002) 'New Labour and the "problem of men"', *Critical Social Policy,* 22(4), pp. 619–641.

Seldon, A. (ed.) (2001) *The Blair Effect: The Blair Government 1997–2001.* London: Little, Brown and Co.

Shah, R. and Hatton, C. (1999) *Caring Alone: Young Carers in South Asian Communities.* London: Barnardos.

Shakespeare, T. (2002) 'Life as a Disabled Child' project, Economic and Social Research Council's 6–16 Programme, Disability Research Unit, University of Leeds and University of Edinborough.

Shakespeare, T. and Watson, N. (1997) 'Defending the social model', in Barton, L. and Oliver, M. (eds) *Disability Studies: Past, Present and Future.* Leeds: The Disability Press.

Showalter, E. (1987) *The Female Malady, Women, Madness and English Culture 1830–1980.* London: Virago.

Simmons, J. *et al.* (2002) *Crime in England and Wales, 2001/2.* London: Home Office Research, Development and Statistics Directorate.

Sinclair, I. and Gibbs, I. (2002) 'Looked after children', in Bradshaw, J. (ed.) *The Well-being of Children in the UK,* London: Save the Children.

Skevik, A. (2003) 'Children of the welfare state: individuals with entitlements or hidden within the family', *Journal of Social Policy,* 32(3), pp. 423–441.

Skinner, C. (2003) 'The social political and welfare context for working with families', in Bell, M. and Stewart, K. (eds) *The Practitioner's Guide to Working with Families.* Basingstoke: Palgrave.

Smart, C. and Neale, B. (1997) 'Good enough morality: divorce and postmodernity', *Critical Social Policy*, 17(4), pp. 3–27.

Smart, C. and Neale, B. (1999) *Family Fragments*. Cambridge: Polity Press.

Smart, C., Neale, B. and Wade, A. (2001) *The Changing Experience of Childhood, Families and Divorce*. Cambridge: Polity.

Smith, C. (ed.) (1998) *Leaving Care: Messages from Young People*. London: RPS Rainer.

Smith, D. (2003) 'New Labour and Youth Justice', *Children & Society*, 17, pp. 226–235.

Smith, D. J. (1997) 'Ethnic Origins, Crime and Criminal Justice', in Maguire, M., Morgan, R. and Reiner, R. (eds) *The Oxford Handbook of Criminology* (2nd Edition). Oxford: Oxford University Press, pp. 703–759.

Smith, J. (2002) Speech to Quality Protects Conference, Birmingham, 20 March.

Smith, R. (2003) *Youth Justice*. Cullompton, Devon: Willan Publishing.

Social Exclusion Unit (1998a) *Truancy and School Exclusion* (Cm 3957). London: The Stationery Office.

Social Exclusion Unit (1998b) *Rough Sleeping* (Cm 4008). London: The Stationery Office.

Social Exclusion Unit (1999) *Teenage Pregnancy* (Cm 4342). London: The Stationery Office.

Social Exclusion Unit (2003) *A Better Education for Children in Care*. London: Social Exclusion Unit.

Social Services Inspectorate (1995) *Young Carers: Something to Think About: Report of Four SSI Workshops May–June 1995*. London: Department of Health.

Social Services Inspectorate (1997) '... When Leaving Home is Also Leaving Care ...', *An Inspection of Services for Young People Leaving Care*. London: Department of Health.

Social Services Inspectorate (1998a) *Social Services Facing the Future: The Seventh Annual Report of the Social Services Inspectorate, 1997/98*. London: The Stationery Office.

Social Services Inspectorate (1998b) *Someone Else's Children: Inspections of Planning and Decision Making for Children Looked After and the Safety of Children Looked After*. London: Department of Health.

Social Services Inspectorate/OFSTED (1995) *The Education of Children Who are Looked After by Local Authorities*. London: HMSO.

Social Trends (2002) *National Statistic Social Trends No. 32*, 2002 Edition. London: The Stationery Office.

Somerville, J. (2000) *Feminism and the Family: Politics and Society in the UK and USA*. Basingstoke: Palgrave.

Stein, M. and Carey, K. (1986) *Leaving Care*. Oxford: Blackwell.

Taylor-Gooby, P. (2003) 'The genuinely liberal genuine welfare state', Paper presented at the Social Policy Association Annual Conference, University of Middlesbrough, 16 July.

The Mental Health Foundation (1999) *Bright Futures*. London: The Mental Health Foundation.

The Mental Health Foundation (2001) 'Turned upside down: developing community-based crisis services for 16–25 year olds experiencing a mental health crisis'. London: The Mental Health Foundation.

Tomlinson, S. (2003) 'New Labour and Education', *Children and Society*. Special Issue, 17(3), June, pp. 195–205.

Toynbee, P. (2003) *Hard Work: Life in Low-Pay Britain*. London: Bloomsbury.

Toynbee, P. and Walker, D. (2001) *Did Things Get Better? An Audit of Labour's Successes and Failures.* London: Penguin Books.

Tunstill, J. (2000) 'Child care', in Hill, M. (ed.) *Local Authority Social Services: An Introduction.* Oxford: Blackwell.

United Nations Committee on the Rights of the Child (1995) *Concluding Observations of the Committee on the Rights of the Child: United Kingdom of Great Britain and Northern Ireland.* (CRC/C/15/Add.34). Geneva: Centre for Human Rights.

United Nations Committee on the Rights of the Child (2002) *Concluding Observations of the Committee on the Rights of the Child: United Kingdom of Great Britain and Northern Ireland.* (CRC/C/15/Add.188 Unedited version). Geneva: Centre for Human Rights.

Utting, W. (1997) *People Like Us: The Report of the Review of Safeguards for Children Living Away from Home.* London: Department of Health/Welsh Office, The Stationery Office.

Waldfogel, J. (1997) *Early Childhood Interventions and Outcomes. CASE Paper 21.* London: London School of Economics.

Wallis, L. and Frost, N. (1998) *Cause for Complaint: The Complaints Procedure for Young People in Care.* London: The Children's Society.

Wassof, F. and Dey, I. (2000) *Family Policy.* Eastbourne, Gildredge.

Waterhouse, R. (2000) *Lost in Care: Report of the Tribunal of Inquiry into the Abuse of Children in Care in the Former County Council Areas of Gwynedd and Clwyd since 1974.* (HC 201). London: The Stationery Office.

Wattam, C. (1999) 'Confidentiality', in Parton, N. and Wattam, C. (eds) *Child Sexual Abuse: Responding to the Experiences of Children.* Chichester: Wiley/NSPCC.

Wattam, C. (2002) 'Making inquiries under Section 47 of The Children Act 1989', in Stewart, K. and James, A. (eds) *The Handbook of Child Protection* (2nd Edition). Harcourt: Bailliere Tindall.

Williams, F. (1989) *Social Policy: A Critical Introduction.* Cambridge: Polity.

Williams, F. (1998) 'Troubled masculinities in social policy discourses: fatherhood', in Popay, J., Hearn, J. and Edwards, J. (eds) *Men, Gender Divisions and Welfare.* London: Routledge.

Williams, F. (1999) 'Good enough principles for welfare', *Journal of Social Policy,* 28(4), pp. 667–689.

Williams, F. (2001) 'In and beyond New Labour: towards a new political ethics of care', *Critical Social Policy,* 21(4), pp. 467–494.

Wilson, K. and James, A. (eds) (2002) *The Child Protection Handbook* (2nd Edition). Harcourt: Tindall.

Winchester, R. (2000) *Listen and Learn in a Chance in Life: Making Quality Protects Happen.* London: Department of Health/Community Care.

Wolmar, C. (2000) *Forgotten Children: The Secret Abuse Scandal in Children's Homes.* London: Vision Paperbacks.

Worcester, R. and Mortimore, R. (2001) *Explaining Labour's Second Landslide.* London: Politico's Publishing.

Wyness, M. G. (2000) *Contesting Childhoods.* London: Falmer Press.

Young Minds (2000a) *Whose Crisis: Meeting the Needs of Children and Young People with Serious Mental Health Problems.* London: Young Minds.

Young Minds (2000b) 'Comment', *Community Care,* 6–12 April, p. 6.

Youth Access (2001) *Breaking Down the Barriers: Key Evaluation Findings on Young People's Mental Health Needs.* London: Youth Access/Department of Health.

Index